the

CHRISTMAS
of '45

the CHRISTMAS *of* '45

MILLS CRENSHAW

BONNEVILLE BOOKS
SPRINGVILLE, UTAH

ISBN 13: 978-1-59955-455-6

Published by Bonneville Books, an imprint of Cedar Fort, Inc., 2373 W. 700 S., Springville, UT 84663
Distributed by Cedar Fort, Inc., www.cedarfort.com

LIBRARY OF CONGRESS CATALOGING-IN-PUBLICATION DATA
   Crenshaw, Mills.
    The Christmas of '45 / Mills Crenshaw.
      p. cm.
    Summary: David, who will turn six on Christmas Day, 1945, touches the hearts of
diverse strangers in his town on Christmas Eve as he seeks help in finding the Savior
to ask Him to return his mother, who recently died.
    ISBN 978-1-59955-455-6
    1. Christmas stories, American--Juvenile fiction. [1. Lost children--Fiction.
2. Faith--Fiction. 3. Christmas--Fiction. 4. Community life--Fiction. 5. Grief--Fiction.
6. Christian life--Fiction. 7. United States--History--1945-1953--Fiction.]
    I. Title. II. Title: Christmas of forty-five.

    PZ7.C86386Chr 2010
    [Fic]--dc22

    2010020559

Cover art by Scott Snow
Cover design by Tanya Quinlain
Cover design © 2010 by Lyle Mortimer
Edited and typeset by Megan E. Welton

Printed in the United States of America

10 9 8 7 6 5 4 3 2 1

Printed on acid-free paper

To all who cherish Christmas, I offer this small gift in
the hope that it will add to the true
Spirit of the season.

For my mother, Thelma Peterson Crenshaw,
who cared enough to correct my English, and my
manners, throughout her ninety-seven years; and for
my children and grandchildren, who provided
the inspiration.

Chapter 1

Morning broke on a scene carved out of alabaster. The pristine powder deposited by the previous night's storm shimmered in the early morning sun. The entire vista was a breathtaking Christmas card. Untouched snow glistened in the foreground before a copse of leafless aspens. In the east, craggy mountain passes beckoned the adventurous with inviting drifts of powder. Seen from the belfry of the Presbyterian Church, the sleeping town lay nestled under its iridescent blanket.

The streets and fields were, as yet, unmarred by the tracks of those who must soon stir from the warmth of their beds. Each home in the valley proudly presented a marshmallow roof laden with nearly two feet of snow. Here and there, half-buried sleds lay in wait for their masters. Lampposts wore ermine top hats, and even the garbage cans were bedecked with a frosty sugar coating.

The North wind seemed to hold its frigid breath in anticipation of greater things to come, but nothing stirred. There was nothing to detract from the ideal Currier & Ives setting.

Then, the spell was broken. Suddenly, the Christmas card transformed into a living tableau as the downtown area sprang to life. The first human efforts were swift and purposeful. Doors opened, and men bearing scrapers, shovels, and brooms attacked the snow that buried their cars as though it was the enemy. They hastily stuffed boxes and packages into backseats or yawning trunks.

They leaped into their respective driver's seats and, with scarcely a glance over their shoulders, they launched their cars into the street, and slipped and slid their way to waiting businesses. They dare not be late—this was not just another business day. It was *the* business day. For many of the town's merchants, the outcome of this day would determine their net profits for the year. This was the dawn of the "Day of the Cash Register." It was Christmas Eve morn.

Young men, dressed as if for the Arctic, began shoveling walks. A snowplow lumbered its way down Main Street, spraying a cascade of snow and ice over cars that were carelessly parked curbside overnight. Homes throughout the town were festooned with evergreen boughs and multicolored lights. Here and there, small red banners hung in windows, displaying a five-pointed blue star on a white background in honor of their loved ones serving in the military. Some had more than one star; others displayed a gold star, indicating their loved one had paid the ultimate price for freedom. For the blue star families, it was a season of joy and anticipation. For the gold star families, it was a season of sorrow.

Midtown, at Famous Fashions Boutique, a young woman Scotch-taped a banner in the window that read, "Giant Christmas Eve Sale—Coats 50% Off." In the background, a tasteful sign read, "Designs Inspired by Edith Head." At the young woman's feet, a fawn-colored pug snored happily, its scrunched snout buried in artificial snow. As a concession to the season, the pedigreed pug had allowed herself to be clothed in a miniature jacket tailored out of Pendleton wool in Saint Andrews tartan. As an added indignity, a red Christmas bow was tied about her neck in place of her regular collar.

Next to the slumbering canine, an animated cat sporting a red and white stocking cap appeared to beckon at passers-by, inviting them to enter and benefit from the last-minute bargains.

The important day's work had begun. After all, this was business! It was important not to let anything interfere with what was becoming the primary purpose of Christmas—profits! This was the first Christmas since the end of the war. It had only been five months since the world had learned about the atomic bomb. The surrender of Japan, the end of rationing, and the return of the troops had come with the suddenness of a whirlwind. Overnight, everything had changed. Austerity had been banished and replaced with a time of plenty. After years of fear and sacrifice, it was time for thanksgiving and celebration. After the prolonged period of self-denial, there were "things" to be had. As if by magic, radios, appliances, and gifts of all kinds suddenly appeared on the shelves. Soon, even new cars would be available again. Darkness had been replaced with glowing, multicolored lights. Costumes of bright red fleece with ermine trim had replaced military olive drab.

In the spirit of Charles Dickens, the past was out of mind, if not forgotten. Everyone worked eagerly to make this Christmas unforgettable.

Chapter 2

Mark paced back and forth in the kitchen as he talked with his sister-in law. The extra long "walkabout" cord had been one of his wife's prized possessions. She loved being able to work in the kitchen at the same time she talked with family and friends on the phone. It had taken Mark more than a month of pleading and letter-writing to get Ma Bell to install the cord. "We can't keep up with demand for installs as it is," the written denials all explained. "We connect nearly 50 percent of the homes in the nation now and demand is growing." But persistence paid off, and his wife had her "walkabout."

"I really appreciate this, Caroline. I can't believe they'd call an emergency meeting on the day before Christmas. Old Scrooge has been spending too much time staring at the company logo." As Mark listened, he walked to the pantry, grabbed a cereal box, a package of raisins, and the elephant-shaped sugar bowl and set them next to his son's place setting. Mark stared at the Wheaties box with the picture of Bob Feller and Lew Fonseca for a moment. Then, remembering, he walked back to the pantry and retrieved the box of the newly popular Cheerioats and added it to the collection.

"No, he's taking it very hard. I'm hoping that going shopping with you will take his mind off of things for a few hours . . . no, I understand, it's been hard on all of us. He'll be ready . . . and Caroline, thank you."

Mark looked down at his sleeping son with a mixture of love and shared anguish. In sleep, the boy was at peace. *I wish I didn't have to wake him,* he thought. Then, softly, he rested his hand on his son's shoulder. He didn't shake the boy; he let the gentle contact call the lad from the healing depths of sleep. There was no reaction.

"Son, wake up." The boy stirred and pulled the goose down quilt tighter around his ears. "Come on, big fella. I know it's early, but you've got to get ready. Your Aunt Caroline is going to pick you up and take you shopping. Breakfast is on the table, and I've got to get to the office.

The covers gave way to a lifted head and a pair of partially opened blue eyes. "Is Mommy coming too?" Then the boy's eyes closed tightly against the involuntary flood of tears, and his small head fell back into his pillow. "I . . . I forgot," came his muffled voice followed by his quiet sobs. After a moment, he rolled on his back and looked at his father. His expression was a mixture of anguish and anger. "Why?" It was an accusation. "I don't understand."

Mark was stricken at his inability to comfort his son. He was torn between the unfeeling demands of work and the emotional needs of his only child. "We'll talk tonight, I promise. Tomorrow is a very important day. It's Christmas, and your birthday."

The boy, now sitting up in bed, slowly shook his head. "I don't want any presents. All I want is Mommy to come home again," he said softly.

Mark sat speechless, searching for something he could say that would ease the pain of his son's loss, which was clearly as agonizing as his own. He settled for reaching out, squeezing the boy on the shoulder, and stumbling out of the room.

In the kitchen, Mark reached for his briefcase, which sat, looking unusually blurry, on the edge of the table. Realizing the cause of the strange sight, Mark wiped away his own tears with his overcoat sleeve, grabbed the case, and headed for the front door. He opened it to a bitter blast of cold air to his face and a furry bump against his ankle.

"Mmeeeooww," Whiskers offered indignantly as she shot past Mark, fresh from her morning constitutional. It wasn't so much a "Thank you, sir, for letting me in," as it was more of a, "Don't you know I was freezing my furry tail off out there?"

But Mark was clearly too deep in thought to notice. He was furious at being commanded to work, and he was troubled that he was unable to answer his son's probing questions when Mark desperately needed those answers himself. He would seek those answers if it was the last thing he did.

Chapter 3

The business day was underway at Liesel's Family Bakery. The walks had been cleared and salted well before dawn. The aroma of freshly baked bread and strudel wafted its way down the block and tempted early risers. One of the boys shoveling sidewalks across the street caught a whiff and suddenly remembered that he hadn't yet had breakfast. He drove his shovel into the snowbank and headed for the kitchen.

Gretchen Liesel was busy putting the finishing touches on a tray of Christmas cookies. There were snowmen and Christmas bells and one cat-faced cookie, topped with a red and white frosting stocking cap.

Though Gretchen wasn't conscious of it, she was every child's picture of a grandmother. Her puffed white sleeves peeked from behind a black lace-up bodice. Her Tyrolean skirt was well protected by a stiffly starched white apron, and her frameless glasses rested comfortably on her nose. It wasn't just the fact that she looked as though she was a character from Disney's *Snow White*—it was more the fact that her genuine love of children radiated from her person like a beacon. And without exception, that love was instantly returned by every child who had the good fortune to find his way into her bakery. "Gramma" Liesel lifted the tray and slid it into a window display.

Gretchen failed to suppress a wistful smile as she relived the Creigthorn family's visit the evening before. The five children circled around her in a perfect stair step, from seven-year-old Stephen to tiny two-year-old Bonnie. They were excited but polite as they each accepted a snowman cookie from their adopted grandmother. But it was little Bonnie who melted Gretchen's heart when she tugged at the older women's apron, wiggled a finger for her to bend down, and whispered, "I love you, Gramma Liesel." Gretchen used a corner of her apron to wipe away a tear at the memory and bustled about the bakery, preparing for the flood of customers soon to fill the shop.

The Liesel bakery was quaint but spotless. There was no sign of spilled flour or uncovered containers that were so typical of American bakeries. Every piece of equipment gleamed. Rolf Liesel stood in the middle of the bakery, polishing an imaginary smudge on the mixer when a timer dinged.

Rolf shut off the mixer and poured its contents into neat rows of pans. He was tall and lean, as fit as many men half his age. He often joked that when he worked for others, he would put in eight full hours a day, but now that he was his own boss, he had cut back to a leisurely fourteen. His spotless white shirt, pants, apron, and baker's hat were carry-overs from his European apprentice days. Even his well-polished, albeit worn, shoes were as white as the flour he used to create delectable pastries. In a well-practice routine, Rolf slid the rack of pans into the oven, reset the timer, and began to wash the huge stainless mixer bowl. No unnecessary motion or task was left for a later moment.

Soft Christmas music played in the background as Rolf carefully dried the bowl. Gretchen joined him and touched his arm affectionately. *Such a good man*, she thought. *Life is good*.

The pleasant Christmas music faded into the background for the morning weather forecast. "You are listening to 'Sounds of Christmas' on AM-1220. Current temperature is thirty-one degrees. The Christmas Eve forecast is for heavy snows, followed by clearing skies and colder temperatures."

Just before the announcer spoke the word "temperatures," the melodic voice of Bing Crosby faded in with his popular Christmas song, "Let It Snow."

Gretchen gave her husband an affectionate hug. He placed the gleaming bowl in the mixer and automatically gave the mechanism a wipe. Then, gently, he put his arms around his wife.

Rolf was an Old World craftsman who had adapted well

to his adopted country. Like many of his European counterparts, he was both well read and well educated. He was a baker by choice and training, not by necessity or circumstance. His slight Austrian accent was part of his considerable charm.

"Is a good thing we get an early start, eh, Mama?"

His wife might have been cast from the same mold. In her day, she had been a beauty. Cultured, refined, and highly respected—that had been before the First World War. Through all the trials of the intervening years, she had aged well. With Rolf by her side, they had weathered everything life had thrown at them. Now, she and her husband were one—even to the accent.

"Such a busy time," she said, turning toward her husband. "All the families—maybe today they'll bring lots of children." She sighed and looked out the window. "Sometimes I still wish," she said, smiling, wistfully expressing an unfulfilled yearning she had voiced a thousand times. "I still wish we could have met when we were young enough for children of our own. But the Lord knows best, *ja*, Papa?"

Rolf tried to comfort his wife but found himself clearing his throat as he turned away and blinked back the tears welling in his own eyes. This was a common discussion spoken many times in their married life.

"It was the war, *Liebchen*. We cannot blame the Lord. Besides, with all the cookies you give the children who come in, we're the honorary *Grosseltern* for half the families in town." In a coaxing voice, he added, "They love you, Mama."

He kissed her on the forehead. "*I* love you, Mama."

Gretchen pretended to be embarrassed. "Behave, you old wolf. Sometimes you are fresher than the bread you bake."

Rolf pulled up a highly polished stool and seated his wife upon it. He then took a seat in front of her. He held her hands in his and patted them gently. "Do you remember when we first met?"

She tilted her head to one side and looked at the corner of the ceiling, conjuring distant memories. "Of course I remember. You looked very funny, standing in that long bread line with all those *hausfrauen*. I was wondering, all the time I watched you, if you were married."

The baker reached over and tugged at the bow of his wife's apron. "I remember that blue apron you wore."

"It was green."

He shrugged and smiled. "Your apron was the only color in that long, drab line of unhappy people."

She placed her hand on the top of his. "And your smile was the only friendly expression in that line. Then they ran out of bread, and I didn't know what I was going to do. Suddenly, this strong man with the warm smile offered to share his bread with me. You were so boastful! 'It's not as good as I bake,' you said."

"It wasn't," he said indignantly. "Besides, soon we were baking together. And I was a happy man for the first time in my life." He cleared his throat and looked away, again blinking hard. "We have shared much that is good, Mama. Working our way across the ocean, baking bread for the Steamship line coming to America—it was an adventure, *ja*? We were blessed, Mama. Think of what our friends went through during the Second War. And now, we have our own bakery and so many new friends. Look at how the world has changed, Mama."

Gretchen nodded and then gave her husband's arm a squeeze. "Who would have thought? It's been good together, *ja*, Papa?"

The baker stood and pulled his wife to her feet. Then he wrapped her in his arms and held her quietly for a moment. "Mama, it has been *wunderbar*, and you are my one true love." For a moment, they were young again. In their hearts and minds, they were still the age they were when they met. Only their outer shells had submitted to the encroachment of time.

Rolf danced an impromptu polka. "And it's Christmas . . . our first real Christmas in so many years."

His enthusiasm made Gretchen laugh quietly.

The old-fashioned bell at the top of the door jangled, announcing the arrival of a customer. Gretchen pulled away, patted her hair, and turned to greet the customer.

The baker smiled wistfully, shook his head a little, and then turned to mark a large calendar on the wall. As he marked an "X" through the date, his wife greeted the first customer of the day.

"Good morning, Mrs. Kartchner! My, but you're getting an early start. . . ."

Chapter 4

At the local precinct, a police lieutenant drew a similar "X" through the same date on a different calendar. This calendar also noted the arrival of Christmas Eve, but underneath it, someone had written "BAH HUMBUG" in bold block letters.

Outside the police station, a light snow fell. At the corner Texaco station, two well-bundled gas attendants were putting out a sign that read, "FULL SERVICE: 17.9¢ per gal." Ever since rationing had ended in August, there had been periodic price wars, but in the shopping rush, no one paid attention to petroleum hostilities. Across the street, a Salvation Army Band lustily rendered, "We Wish You a Merry Christmas." Early shoppers bustled past. Some dropped coins in the kettle, but most seemed preoccupied and rushed. Two boys on opposite sides of the street were waging a snowball fight. Part of the game was to launch their missiles between passing cars, ducking behind the next passing vehicle to rearm. Street noise rose with the increasing frenzy of last minute shopping. A redheaded boy, who wore his dad's bomber jacket, packed an oversized projectile and waited for an opening in the traffic. When the opportunity came, he let the snowball fly. He missed his opponent and hit the tuba player. The musician burped a sour note and started to his feet. Luckily for the boy, the musician remembered who he was and what he was doing out in the cold. He settled his ruffled dignity back on the chair and resumed playing.

Inside the police station, the desk sergeant attempted to do several things at once. He shuffled reports and attempted to answer the phone while checking off the roster at shift change. None of the tasks were finished with any degree of success. He had neatly arranged three black dial phones on the raised counter before him. In frustration, he kept glancing over his shoulder at the plug-in switchboard, visible through the sliding glass window directly behind him. He was convinced the station operators overloaded him with calls just for sport.

The station was well lit and well organized. There was none of the clutter or accumulated grime so prevalent in big city station houses. This was due, in part, to Sergeant Kim's fanatic devotion to organization and also to the fact that the mayor's office and city council chambers were housed on the second floor of the same building. That the mayor happened to be the local GE distributor was a happy coincidence that proved the major contributing factor to the brightly lit ambience of the station. His Honor had successfully convinced the city council that installing GE's new Circlin Fluorescent fixtures would, as he said, "put the maximum amount of light in the smallest space." He had also made a major point of the fact that, at only twenty-two watts each, the city would save significant amounts on their electric bill. There was no question that the new fixtures had noticeably brightened the station house. They had also contributed significantly to the mayor's bank balance.

As the desk sergeant routinely handled the calls, the volume of traffic in the station house increased. Officers passed by, some showed him their clipboards, and Kim nodded as he marked them off the roster. Others handed him forms to sign, which he did perfunctorily. Others waved and engaged fellow officers in conversation.

The center phone rang once, and the sergeant snatched the handset out of its cradle with his left hand as he signed a proffered clipboard with his right.

"Police Department, Sergeant Kim. How may I help you?" He listened for a moment and scowled as his patience wore thin. He paused a second longer as he listened to the person on the other end of the line. "No, no . . . 'scuse me, ma'am . . . Animal Control handles barking dogs, Jackson 5-2700." He rolled his eyes at the ceiling and repeated very slowly. "That's J-A-5. Yes, ma'am, five two five . . . no, not

JACKSON-525 . . . err, it's JACKSON 5. Yes, ma'am, 525"
He clenched his teeth and said still louder, "5-2-5 . . . No, I
was not shouting, ma'am."

Officer Bob Slovak entered the station house with two
prisoners in handcuffs and presented himself before the desk
sergeant. Slovak had been back from the war less than six
months, but he had already won the respect of his superiors
and a degree of resentment from some of the less professional
and less productive members of the force. Slovak was young,
big, ramrod straight, and hard as nails. His military service
was evident by his posture and precise movements. His prisoners appeared to be a little old lady and Santa Claus. Several of the officers stopped in their tracks to gawk.

Detective Branagen sneered as he passed and added
snidely, "Hey, Big Bob, you buckin' for lieutenant? This bust
is going to look great on your report!" Branagen was as big as
Slovak, but not nearly as fit. The extra twenty pounds he carried protruded over his Sam Brown belt, and the veins in his
bulbous nose testified that his after-hours exercise of choice
was bending the elbow. He was one of those who resented
Slovak's spit-and-polish military attitude.

Slovak's scowl sent Branagen scurrying out of harm's
way. The desk sergeant stood for a moment, his mouth
slightly agape. He held up a hand, stopping Slovak where he
stood. Then, fighting for control, he finished his conversation. "That's right ma'am, you've got it. 2-7-0-0. No, ma'am,
no trouble a-tall."

The desk sergeant slammed the phone down and muttered under his breath. Looking up, he snapped, "This is a joke, right, Slovak? I'm going home tonight and telling the kids that I booked a little old lady and Santa Claus on Christmas Eve."

Officer White stopped in mid-stride to observe the spectacle. White fancied himself a wit and was tolerated primarily because he stood six feet five inches tall, weighed 290 pounds, and was capable of subduing the most obnoxious drunks and felons in the house. He was also a bit of a loudmouth. He had a deep bass voice and a proclivity for making jokes at other officers' expense. White motioned to some officers, who were exiting the squad bay, to gather round.

"Somebody call the FBI!" White shouted in mock alarm. "Sherlock Holmes here has single-handedly captured the 'Claus' Gang!"

Officer Bush, one of the oldest members of the force, who had nearly put in his twenty, laughed as he joined the growing crowd. "You're going to be famous, Slovak! I can see the headlines now—'The Man Who Busted Santa Claus!' "

"Hey, I like that," Officer Decker piped up. "There ought to be a reward or somethin'. Whaddaya say, guys?"

Slovak did a slow burn as other officers joined in the spoof. They gathered around, out of both amusement and curiosity. Sergeant Kim looked on with resignation at this obvious breakdown in station discipline.

By now, other officers and staff had joined the crowd in

an effort to find out what was going on. Some shook their heads, others laughed out loud, but most just enjoyed the spectacle.

Slovak had had enough and shoved his prisoners forward. Cynically he barked, "Ho! Ho! Ho!"

Sergeant Kim rolled his eyes and gestured at the sky with both hands as if to say, "Why me?" By now, the crowd of bystanders had grown significantly.

The sergeant held up his hands for quiet. Then, with resignation, he said, "All right, all right . . . I suppose I've got to hear this. What have public enemies numbers one and two done to terrorize the city?"

Slovak, with a wry smile, centered the little old lady in front of the sergeant's desk. "Meet Charles Thurgood the Second, a.k.a. 'Charlie the Cannon.' Tip your hat to the sergeant, Chuck."

Slovak ripped off the old lady's wig. The makeup was now apparent, and Charlie looked indignant. "I want to call my lawyer."

The desk sergeant nodded knowingly. "All in good time, Chucky m'boy. All in good time." He picked up the phones, which had been ringing in unison. One after the other he answered them, and then set each receiver on the desk, effectively placing the callers on hold. "Police Department, please hold. Police Department, please hold."

The sergeant nodded his head toward Santa, as if awaiting the second act of this little play. Slovak shoved Charlie aside and then centered Santa. He untied the big red sack and loosened the top but did not disclose the contents quite yet.

Slovak played to the crowd, as he offered an informal report. "As you will recall from our morning briefing, we were told to be on the lookout for a team of pickpockets working with good ol' Charlie. We were told that Charlie never holds. After lifting a wallet, he always passes off to one or more of his highly trained associates. We were also told that they usually have some gimmick—something that makes it tough to follow the handoff. Let me introduce Nick Kassky, a.k.a. 'Saint Nick.' Nicky, here, came up with this year's prize-winning magic."

Slovak lifted Santa's sack and dumped its contents onto the desk—an assortment of wallets, money clips, and purses. The bystanders were either amused, impressed, or shaking their heads in disbelief.

Sergeant Kim raised one eyebrow. "My, but you've been busy little elves." Then to Slovak, matter-of-factly, he ordered, "Book 'em." There was a smattering of applause, and the onlookers dispersed.

"Oh, and Slovak?"

Slovak had started to turn away. He waited for the other shoe to fall. "Yeah, Sarge?"

The sergeant smiled sweetly. "As a reward for your 'outstanding service' to the community, you've been assigned overtime tonight. The merchants have asked for extra patrols and traffic control." He picked up the third phone. "Police Department, please hold."

Slovak reacted as if in great pain. "Hey, Sarge, gimme a break!"

Sergeant Kim ignored him and turned back to the phones. "Sorry, Slovak. The merchants tell the mayor, the mayor tells the brass, the brass tells me, I tell you, and you get to take it out on little old ladies . . . and Santa." Sergeant Kim then grabbed the first phone and barked, "Thank you for holding. Sergeant Kim, how may I help you?"

Slovak wheeled his prisoners about, headed for the door marked "Holding Cells," and called back over his shoulder, "Just another reason why I hate Christmas!"

Chapter 5

Whiskers was a very determined cat. She propelled her tiger-striped body down the hall, pausing only momentarily at her young master's bedroom door. Cautiously, she stuck her nose around the partially opened door, hesitated for a second, and then pushed her way into the room. She hesitated once again, sniffing the air before gathering herself and leaping to the top of the dresser. There she found the remains of a tuna sandwich, which she proceeded to devour.

The dresser was covered with an assortment of treasures that only a small boy could appreciate. In the left-most corner was a recent picture of the little boy and his mother. In the picture, the boy's mother had her arm around his shoulder. He was holding a teddy bear dressed in a Christmas costume. The boy smiled up at her. Next to the picture was a memorial program with a picture of the same woman with an inscription which read, "In loving memory." The program was partly covered by a baseball mitt in which rested a well-scuffed ball. Next to the mitt was a jar of pennies, a small pocketknife, three well-polished pebbles, a wrapped piece of bubble gum, and a piece of string. There were several old prints of long-departed relatives mounted in antique photo frames. One of the pictures was of a period wedding. The bride was young and beautiful, dressed in a simple white dress. Over her head and shoulders was draped a shawl of delicate Irish lace. She and her new husband stood in front of a gray granite structure. There was a small brass nameplate at the base. Next to the family portrait was a thick, two-post binder labeled "Family Genealogy."

Whiskers was unimpressed with these treasures. She had finished her snack and moved carefully through the collection to the edge of the dresser. She hung her tawny head over the edge, carefully judged the distance, dropped to the bed below, and landed beside a sleeping boy.

David, Whisker's master, was six years old, or would be on Christmas Day. He was blond, with a tousled shock of hair over his eyes. He was fully dressed in jeans, sneakers, and a light blue jacket, but he slept deeply. After getting dressed, David had drifted off again, his head slightly hanging over the edge of the bead. The Christmas bear, shown in the picture Whiskers had carefully skirted, was snuggled next to him. The bear was dressed for the season in a red and white stocking cap, a green parka, and miniature snow boots. A candy cane was in its right paw. A small wallet rested in the boy's open hand. Whiskers began to purr noisily and then nuzzled the boy, finally sticking her nose in the boy's ear.

David turned away from the wet nose and sleepily demanded, "Go 'way Whiskers . . . stop it . . . darn cat." Slowly, he became more alert, rose up on one elbow, and sadly drew the cat next to him. His eyes filled with tears, and he dropped his head back on the bed. Sadly, he accepted reality. "I dreamed that Mommy was here . . . she was holding me and reading to me, just like she used to . . . but she's gone, Whiskers. My mommy's gone."

In the distance, a door opened and closed. David's Aunt Caroline called down the hall, "David, are you ready? We're burning daylight."

David sat up and wiped his eyes. He stuffed his wallet in his jacket pocket as his Aunt Caroline appeared at the door, knocked lightly, and peered into his room. She resembled the boy's mother, though their hairstyle and color differed slightly. Whiskers jumped off the bed and proceeded to wrap herself around Aunt Caroline's legs.

"Ready to go, big fella? It's going to be brutal out there. All those last-minute shoppers are getting in the way of our last-minute shopping—how dare they! No, Whiskers, you can't come. Begging will get you nowhere." She looked carefully at her nephew and bit her lower lip as she tried to think of some way to cheer him up. "I don't know about your dad. Do you think he really had an urgent business meeting, or do you think he was just trying to get out of going shopping with us?"

David shrugged. Caroline painted on a smile and, with false cheerfulness, clapped her hands. "Well then, let's do it!"

David nodded in resignation, propped the Christmas bear on his pillow, and gave Whiskers a parting pat.

Chapter 6

Rick McSwain hung his headset over the microphone stand at Talk Radio AM-1220. With a flourish, he signed the log as required at the end of his shift. Fellow talk show host, Kelly Green, tilted back in the guest chair next to him, awaiting the transfer of power at the change of shift. Actually, tonight's changeover came mid-shift, since Kelly had agreed to cover the rest of Rick's allotted time. The studio was Spartan at best. A large circular clock relentlessly marked time while the station log lay open by the mike, awaiting Kelly's signature. The studio monitor had been turned down so the two could talk over the Christmas music playing in the background.

In his broad but cultured Irish brogue, Rick tried to sound sincere as he offered, "I really appreciate your bailing me out of here, good buddy. I'm no disk jockey, for Pete's sake! Imagine me playing one bloody Christmas carol after another! I'd be bored out of my socks inside an hour."

Rick replaced his head set on his curly shock of red hair and held up his hand as the Christmas carol ended. He leaned into the microphone and intoned with his on-air voice, "You're listening to 'Sounds of Christmas' on AM-1220. A special presentation for our regular talk show listeners . . . ."

He hit the "mute" button. "Who was the genius who thought this up?" Then, releasing the "mute" button, he added, "We will resume regular talk-programming at noon tomorrow." Muting the station, he continued, "Right, they can call in and tell us about their divorce, their drunken Aunt Sally who disgraced herself at the family party, a robbery, or even a bloody homicide."

Rick killed the mike and leaned back in his studio swivel chair. Kelly was having a hard time restraining his laughter.

Rick, feigning a BBC newsreader's presentation, continued, "The major story at the moment is the huge storm bearing down on the valley. The weather service warns that last-minute shopping could be hazardous, as the front is expected to dump up to two feet of snow in a period of just a few hours. If you have anything to buy, you'd better get cracking! Oh, very important—you'll want to make plans to protect our furry friends. The cold front behind the storm is expected to send temperatures plummeting below zero before morning.

"Well, good friends, I'm off to join the madding crowd

and arm wrestle a little old lady for that last-minute gift. My colleague Kelly Green . . . ."

He hit the "mute" button again, "Where did you come up with that name?" He released the button and continued, " . . . will continue with the 'Sounds of Christmas.' So, until tomorrow, this is Rick McSwain wishing you a very merry Christmas!"

Rick hit the "play" button to start the next carol and relinquished his seat. Kelly slid into position and plugged in his headset. Rick wrapped the cord around his own set and stowed it in his locker.

"I really appreciate this, old man. Another three hours of Christmas music, and I'd be round the bend."

Kelly waved it off. "No problem." He checked the music levels, signed the log and then, as an afterthought, turned back to Rick. "Uh, Rick, just don't forget, you're covering for me on New Year's Eve. And before you leave, deposit a six-pack of Pepsi in the fridge, all right?"

Kelly then drank deeply from the bottle he held and finished it with obvious satisfaction.

Rick wrinkled his nose in mock disgust. "Have you ever thought about joining one of those twelve-step programs, Pepsi Anonymous, or somethin' like that? The next thing we know, you'll be robbing little old ladies to pay for your habit."

Kelly scowled. "Whaddaya talkin' about? They're only a nickel."

Rick made a big show of looking for something. He opened cabinets and tilted chairs to look under them.

Kelly squinted at him. "Looking for something?"

Rick nodded vigorously. "Yeah, I'm looking for your hidden stash. We can't have you getting drunk on Pepsi while you're on the air."

Kelly grabbed a fistful of Pepsi bottle caps and threw them at Rick.

Chapter 7

The streets of the community had undergone a change of character. The crush of shoppers had intensified and so had the weather. People seemed far more rushed and far less tolerant as they shoved their way toward store entrances. As if to match their mood, the sky darkened. One by one, the streetlights and decorations came to life.

The entrance to the Main Street Toy Store was brightly lit and inviting. An outdoor speaker played Bing Crosby's "White Christmas." The windows on both sides of the toy store's arched entryway boasted elaborate, mechanized Christmas scenes. On the left, a mechanical Santa worked in his shop. He held a headless doll in his hand and swung back and forth, looking for the missing part. At the foot of his stool, a playful puppy held the doll's head in its mouth. Each time Santa swung to one side or the other, the puppy scampered to the other side. Santa's elves were busily assembling toys, while one nearsighted elf with thick glasses seemed to be disassembling them.

The opposite window display featured a family of mechanized polar bears. One large bear rode a unicycle back and forth on a high wire. Two cubs dangled precariously from opposite ends of the balance pole. A third cub rode on the large bear's back, with his hands covering the rider's eyes. Other bears were busily climbing up and down a giant candy cane. One cub was eating honey out of a hive, while angry bees chased yet another cub around a rock. The speaker outside this display window played "March of the Toy Soldiers."

As Caroline and David approached the store, they walked together but were in two different worlds. Caroline was tired, and her feet ached. David was curious about everything. He was just one of many youngsters gazing longingly at the endless array of toys. His lightweight blue jacket seemed a little out of place among the other children, who were bundled up against the increasing cold. David put his face up against the window and watched the display. He was mesmerized.

A clerk inside the store watched David's reaction to the Christmas display through the store window. The boy fascinated her for a moment, but then she turned back to her customers who demanded her undivided attention.

Caroline leaned down to match David's height and smiled in wonder at the tableau. She stood captivated for a moment, and then looked at her nephew. With a jerk of her head, she signaled for him to follow and led the way inside.

The shelves were piled high with toys of every kind. An elaborate electric train wound its way through a miniature landscape. The train captured the attention of almost every dad who came within whistle range of the store. These oversized "boys" were packed so tightly around the diorama that their offspring found great difficulty squeezing into a position that gave them a glimpse of the electric marvel.

Caroline dropped, exhausted, onto a bench. She arranged the packages she had been carrying to one side, brushed at a curl that drooped at her forehead, snatched off a shoe, and vigorously massaged her foot. Her face took on an air of ecstasy. David climbed onto the seat next to her and studied his aunt intently.

Caroline gave a long sigh. "Oh . . . oh . . . o-h-h-h!" She continued to rub for a moment and then slumped in exhaustion.

David lost interest in his aunt and moved on to study a collection of oversized stuffed animals. Deep in thought, David's vision blurred slightly. At that moment, the stuffed menagerie took on an almost magical character. In the boy's imagination, the plush animals began dancing. They seemed to perform just for him, as though they were his own personal pets.

Caroline sat up and rubbed her eyes. She felt dazed as she looked at the animals. "I really must be beat . . . dozed off . . . you wouldn't believe the dream. . . ." She looked at David and then at the animals. "You didn't . . . ?" David looked at his aunt curiously. She shook her head "No, of course not."

Caroline noticed that her nephew was watching her strangely, but she couldn't stop rubbing her foot. Still exhausted, she switched feet. "Ah . . . well, almost done. You're lucky. Santa takes care of your presents, so you don't have to go through all this." Then she realized he *was* going through "all this." "Um, well, tomorrow, it'll all be over. Look, I've got a couple of things I need to get here. You stay and watch the train, all right? I'll just be in the back of the store, but no peeking, okay?"

David shrugged and hung his head for a moment. Then he looked at his aunt intently. "Aunt Caroline, can I ask you something?"

She looked at her nephew warily. "Of course."

David hesitated, as though he wasn't exactly sure how to phrase the question, and then plunged ahead. "You and my mom were good friends, weren't you? I mean, besides being sisters an' everything? She'd tell you lots of things, right?"

"We were the closest of friends, David. And yes, she'd share things. I don't think we had any secrets from each other."

The boy searched her face as if to find his answer there. "Then why did she go to live with Jesus? That's what everybody says."

Caroline was startled by the question. "Well, she was very sick . . . ."

David started crying softly. "But we need her. . . . *I* need her. If I went to Jesus and told him that tomorrow is my birthday too but that I don't need any birthday presents or Christmas presents or anything, just my mom to be with us to take care of us and hold me and sing to me like she used to, would he let her come home?"

Caroline looked away, fighting for composure. "I . . . well . . . David, it's difficult to explain. I think you need to talk with your dad about this, okay? Then, if you still want to, we'll talk some more about it."

Disappointed, David looked at the ground and nodded. *Why is it*, he thought, *that big people won't talk about the really important questions?*

Caroline looked at her watch and then at her shopping list. "Ouch, we're almost out of time. I'm just going to go find a few things I need and we'll go. . . . I shouldn't be more than ten, maybe fifteen, minutes. You stay right here or over there by the train, okay? And remember, no peeking!" Looking at her nephew with concern, she added, "Will you be okay? I'll be right here with you in the store."

David, still disappointed, nodded and looked away.

Caroline gathered up her packages and turned to leave. "I'll hurry right back."

David looked around slowly. As he turned, he noticed the shoppers scurrying by. People were everywhere. Most carried packages, and almost all seemed to be in a hurry. Some were happy, and some seemed harassed, but they all were oblivious to the sad little boy. For David, the season and its festivities were rendered meaningless by the loss of his mother. Listlessly, David wandered around the front of the toy shop.

Suddenly, he found himself standing toe to toe with a giant teddy bear. The bear looked down at him benevolently. Instinctively, David reached out and shook its hand. The bear seemed to nod at the boy. The encounter did nothing to soften his melancholy. David then moved to the window that had a display of moving mannequins representing Santa's elves. They were operating a "Rube Goldberg" device that spit out toys and presents. This fascinated the boy for a moment. He moved outside the doorway to get a better look.

The outdoor speakers played "Hark the Herald Angels Sing." A lady wearing a sandwich sign that read, "Liesel's Family Bakery," passed by and handed David a sample cookie. With thanks, he accepted the offering, popped it in his mouth, and continued to look around. A strolling group of carolers, dressed in old-fashioned Dickens-period attire, approached. David took a seat on a bench and listened.

The carolers, in perfect harmony, sang "What Child Is This."

What child is this, who laid to rest;
On Mary's lap is sleeping?

Whom Angels greet with anthems sweet,
While shepherds watch are keeping?

The carolers were exceptional. Immediately, a crowd gathered around. Though he didn't understand why, David noticed a deep wave of longing produced by the carolers and their old fashioned rendition. David had a hard time seeing the singers, so he stood on tiptoe on the bench.

This, this is Christ the King
Who shepherds guard and Angels sing.
Haste, haste to bring him laud,
The babe, the son of Mary.

The carolers moved on, singing a traditional salutation:

We wish you a Merry Christmas,
We wish you a Merry Christmas,
We wish you a Merry Christmas,
And a Happy New Year!

David followed the carolers for several steps, and then he came to a stop in front of a furniture store's display window. All of the stores seemed to be competing for his attention. And at that moment, the lights in the window before him brightened to reveal a domestic Christmas scene. A mannequin mother held a lifelike boy on her lap and rocked him before an artificial fireplace on which hung traditional stockings. The mother appeared to be reading from an oversized book labeled *Christmas Stories*. An animated cat looked over the mother's shoulder. The cat turned its head from side to side and twitched its mechanical tail. In the background, an oversized mechanical mouse stuck its head up out of one of the stockings. As the cat looked its way, the mouse hid back inside its stocking.

David was overcome by the scene. He stood frozen in place long enough to take in the display, but then he covered his eyes as though wiping away tears and turned and propelled himself into the rush of shoppers. Everywhere he turned, he was confronted with scenes that reminded him of joyous times with his mother. But now, each of these encounters reopened the painful realization of his loss. He saw a mother seated on a bench, her arm around her son. They were talking—she gave her son a squeeze, and David turned away. He ran into another mother and son walking hand in hand. He turned away again. He saw a line of people waiting to see Santa. There were mothers with their daughters, but for him the mothers and sons were highlighted to the point that they were the only people he saw. He turned away once again and was confronted by a woman and son standing before another elaborate window display depicting the birth of Christ. David moved closer.

The woman hugged her son and pointed toward the display, explaining, "We give gifts at Christmas to celebrate his birthday. But don't ever forget—his life, and what he did for us, was the greatest gift of all. That's the true meaning of Christmas. Always remember, he's our friend." The woman and son walked away from the window. David no longer heard them. He moved to the window and stared at the crèche. He heard echoes of his own mother's voice in his mind. *Don't ever forget, David, this was the greatest gift of all. When we need help, we ask in his name. . . . He is our friend. . . .*

Filled with a new dedication, David moved back into the flow of shoppers and searched the faces of those who passed by. One busy man approached, walking briskly. David tried to match his stride but couldn't. He ran to catch up.

David tugged at the man's sleeve, "Excuse me, sir, where can I find Jesus?"

The busy man didn't break his stride. He looked down at the boy incredulously. Annoyed, he snapped, "What?"

David stopped trying to keep pace. His shoulders sagged in discouragement. He came to a stop in front of an extremely beautiful woman with deep auburn hair.

There was something about her that David found captivating. She smiled warmly at him. She was dressed totally in white. Her dress was elegant but reminiscent of another era. The high neck and full-length sleeves were inset with lace and fastened with lace loops over small round pearls. Over her head and shoulders was an exquisite shawl of delicate Irish lace. Her shoes were basic white pumps. When David stopped, the woman seemed to be surrounded in brilliant blue-white light. The other shoppers faded from David's view. No one else seemed to notice David or the beautiful woman.

She spoke softly to him, "You have to search for him."

David didn't understand. "Pardon me?"

The woman's smile was undiminished. "If you search for the friend you seek, you will find him."

David studied her for a moment. Slowly, his face brightened with understanding and excitement. He glanced at the crowd, and then turned back. The woman had vanished. Nearby, where the two had been standing, there was a small Christmas tree with a pure white angel on top.

Chapter 8

At the gift-wrap counter, an enormous line wound its way well back into the store. Weary shoppers leaned against the wall, and younger shoppers sat hunched in clumps on the floor. Father Powell had worked his way forward until, finally, he was second in line. People kept glancing his way.

It wasn't so much that he was a member of the clergy; it was more that he was a rather large man with well-chiseled features. His dark hair was salted with grey that had gone white at the temples. More than one woman thought it was a pity that this handsome man was a man of the cloth. His black wool coat was still buttoned against the cold that waited outside the store. And even though his white woolen muffler had loosened slightly, revealing his collar, Father Powell was still uncomfortably warm. Unfortunately, a large stack of unwrapped gifts in his arms prevented him from shedding his coat.

As the overweight shopper in front of him paid, she rummaged through a rather large handbag, looking for exact change. Slowly and carefully, she counted the coins, and then meticulously arranged each gift in a sack. Father Powell looked over his shoulder in ill-disguised impatience. The faces that stared back were all but bereft of any vestige of human kindness.

At last, the shopper in front of him moved out of line. Father Powell placed his stack on the counter and heaved an audible sigh of relief. He glanced at his watch and groaned inwardly at the loss of time.

The gift-wrap clerk was tired, overworked, and short-tempered. She was sharp-faced and totally devoid of the Christmas spirit. Not even looking at her customer, she asked perfunctorily, "Help you?"

Father Powell sighed again and removed his muffler. He looked over the display of wrapped boxes one last time. "Yes, thank you. Let's see . . . I think . . . yes! The teddy bear wrap for the toys and that beautiful gold foil for this." Father Powell held out a thin, flat jewelry box. The clerk grabbed the box, examined it carefully, and tilted her head, giving him a questioning look.

"That's the dollah seventy-five wrap, you know."

Father Powell examined the clerk more closely. He was both annoyed and amused. Unconsciously, he started stroking his right eyebrow between the first finger and thumb of his right hand. He'd been victim to this nervous habit since his youth—it was something he did whenever he was irritated or in deep thought.

"Yes, well . . . it's perfectly all right. It's for my mother."

The clerk sniffed. Swiftly and efficiently, she arranged the boxes. She was almost mechanical in her work, yet artful. Not a movement was wasted. Her effortless skill was a ballet for the hands.

Overhead, the store played a rhythmic Christmas tune that seemed perfectly suited to the worker's motions. Father Powell watched the clerk with detached fascination. Absently he asked, "Busy night?"

The clerk didn't miss a beat or raise her head, but the look she gave him out of the corner of her eye could have withered flowers.

Suddenly sheepish, Father Powell looked around. Again, he twisted and stroked his right eyebrow. He looked at the line of shoppers behind him. They too seemed impatient. Some looked at their watches, some shifted packages, and others just glowered. In the background, the little boy named David passed unnoticed.

The clerk finished wrapping the gold foil package. Father Powell watched her with genuine admiration. "Say, you're really good!"

The clerk placed the gold foil package on top of the other wrapped packages. She was about to hand the stack to Father Powell when he observed, "This store is really lucky to have you." She paused for an instant and seemed to soften ever so slightly. She reached into a bin, pulled out a small gold bell with a gold ribbon, and affixed it to the gold foil package. With just a hint of a smile, she extended the finished stack of packages toward Father Powell.

"For your mother. Merry Christmas."

A light snow started falling. On the street corner, a Salvation Army worker stood in the cold, patiently ringing a bell. Little David exited the store, hesitated, looked up at the snow, and hunched his shoulders as he shuffled off into the crowd of shoppers streaming along the sidewalk.

As he moved through the crowd, David was pushed and shoved by big people totally oblivious of his presence. All around him, people crowded in, their packages banging into him. Soon, David was lost in the swirling crowd. It had become an indistinguishable mass, and David was nowhere to be seen.

Aunt Caroline returned to the entrance of the toy store only to find David missing. Frantic, she searched throughout the store, but saw no sign of her nephew. In desperation, she tried to catch the attention of a cashier. "Excuse me, ma'am? Please, can you help me?"

Annoyed, the cashier gave her a fleeting glance and motioned for her to go to the end of the line. Several shoppers looked at her with varying levels of hostility.

Caroline refused to be deterred. "Have you seen a little boy . . . light blue coat . . . he was waiting right here."

The cashier was tired, irritated, and out of sorts, "Lady, I've seen hundreds of little boys today, and they all look alike to me."

Caroline turned away in frustration and renewed her search. She moved from shop to shop, looking through their windows in the vain hope of finding him there. After a little while, she stood helpless in a stream of shoppers. Not knowing which way to turn, Caroline uttered a silent prayer and turned to find herself standing in front of a woman dressed in white. The woman smiled at her. Caroline, focused on her quest, nodded perfunctorily, and turned away to search the crowd.

"May I help you?"

Caroline spun to face the woman she had just ignored. The woman's features were smooth and unblemished. Her skin was like alabaster. Her bright, intelligent eyes were exceptionally alert.

"Beg your pardon?" Caroline asked, confused. "Oh! Yes, please. Have you seen—?"

"A little boy in a light blue jacket?" the woman responded kindly.

Caroline was surprised. "Yes! How did you—"

Still smiling, the women pointed toward the exit. "He left. He's searching for the Savior."

Caroline looked at the woman in disbelief. "*What?*"

The woman suddenly grew serious. "He had something important to ask . . . before Christmas comes."

Caroline stared at the woman for a moment and turned to go in the direction indicated, but she hesitated. "How do you know?"

She turned back, only to find the woman had disappeared. Caroline looked all around, but the woman was not to be seen.

Knowing she had waited too long to find the little boy on her own, Caroline decided she ought to call Mark—maybe even the police.

Caroline saw a pay phone partway down the walk and rushed over. The man using the phone deliberately turned his back as she approached and closed the folding glass door. Caroline tried the adjacent phone only to discover it was out of order. Her frustration mounting, she walked back to the first phone booth and pounded on the door.

The man on the phone turned around, glowered at her, and turned his back again. The middle-aged caller was casually dressed and acted as though he had all the time in the world.

"Really? I shoulda known . . . you're one of the luckiest people I've ever met." He paused, looked at his fingernails, and then responded, "Naw, nothing special . . . ."

Caroline walked around to the side of the booth to confront the man again. She yelled through the glass, "Excuse me! I've got an emergency!"

Annoyed, the man tried to turn his back again. Caroline moved to the front of the booth and slammed her shoulder into the folding door, partly opening it. The caller was rattled but continued talking. "Oh, I just thought I'd call you up for old times—" He covered the mouthpiece with his hand and snarled at Caroline, "Hey! Whaddaya think you're doing?"

By now, Caroline was the personification of cold fury. "I've got a genuine emergency. If you're not off that phone in ten seconds, I'll start screaming 'Police!' loud enough to attract every security man from here to—"

"Okay, okay. Good grief, lady." The caller was torn between his anger at being interrupted and his fear that Caroline intended to do exactly what she threatened. He spoke into the telephone receiver "Uh, let me call you back in a minute, okay? Somebody's got an emergency."

Caroline grabbed the phone out of the man's hand before he could get out of the way. She shoved a nickel in the slot and dialed a number. Partway through dialing, she realized she had made a mistake, slammed the receiver on the hood, dug the nickel out of the coin return, and started again. By now, she was near tears. She spoke urgently to the party at the other end of the phone. "This is an emergency!"

Chapter 9

Mark, stood at the front of the boardroom of the Fuel Miser company. From his position at the head of the conference table, he looked out at the executives staring back at him from both sides of the boat-shaped slab. Sweat trickled down his back as he cleared his throat and tried again to hammer home the point that was central to his presentation. He tapped the wooden pointer on the graph that indicated sales trends on a growth chart. On either side of the chart were sales posters showing an attractive array of gasoline-powered lawn mowers. Above the mowers, an illustration of Scrooge scowled down at him. The skinflint was pouring coins in his pocket purse. Below the rendering was the company trademark, "Fuel Miser."

"So, in spite of an industry-wide downturn, we've increased our total market share by 2.3 percent." Mark turned to the assembled executives and forcefully reiterated his point.

The five executives were in various stages of stupor. Their posture reflected the fact that they had been at this for some time. Most were in shirtsleeves, cuffs rolled up. To his left sat the new brand manager, Karen Thornton. Karen was a distaff copy of the other execs. Her tailored business jacket hung over the back of her chair. Her striped blouse was open at the throat and, instead of a tie, she wore a simple strand of pearls. Except for those concessions to femininity, she might as well have been wearing a company uniform.

During the war, while other women were taking jobs on the munitions assembly lines, Karen had won her spurs in administration. She had sworn to herself that she would never become just another "Rosie the Riveter." Karen shifted her position in an attempt to hide her boredom. There was an assortment of notepads with pages turned back, cups, glasses, and carafes of water and pots of coffee, all of which were nearly empty. At the opposite end of the table from Mark, the company president leaned forward, taking notes. On his right, Frank, the assistant marketing director, looked skeptically at his notes.

Frank was envious of Mark's history of success. That envy most often surfaced as hostility in corporate meetings. "Yes, but your department had a 10 percent increase in the advertising budget to work with. Unless my notes are inaccurate, you forecast substantial growth."

A secretary entered and quietly spoke to the company president. His reaction showed he was unhappy with her message. She made another comment, shrugged, and then left.

Mark responded to Frank patiently, as though speaking to a child. "Yes, Frank, but no one in the industry anticipated the sharp seasonal downturn following the end of the war. We're one of the few firms that continued to grow—"

The president held up his hand to stop the conversation. He was clearly unhappy at the interruption. With exaggerated patience, he issued a rebuke. "In spite of my instructions not to be disturbed, you have a phone call, Mark. They say it's urgent." He smiled grimly to show he didn't believe it.

Mark moved to pick up the telephone, but his boss held up a hand. Then, for everyone's benefit, he said, "We're fighting for our economic life here. Asking everyone to spend half a day working on Christmas Eve, planning a campaign that can give us a jump on the competition hardly qualifies me as Scrooge, now does it? Particularly since it's all of your jobs that are at stake. The sooner we get this meeting over with, the sooner we can all get home to the parties. Are we clear?"

Everyone glanced at his or her watch or at the wall clock that read 4:45 p.m. Everyone was incredulous at the reference to "half a day's" work. Karen glanced at the president, and, seeing he wasn't looking at her, she gave Mark a sympathetic shrug. The boss waved his hand imperiously while Mark picked up the black receiver.

"Yes?" He rubbed his forehead as he listened. "Have you checked with security?" The president's impatience grew by the moment. He clenched his jaw and shook his head at the other executives as if to say, "Can you believe this?" Mark glanced his way, bit his lower lip, and then looked down at the phone.

"You stay wherever you are. I'll get there as soon as I can. And Caroline . . . it's going to be all right." He paused, listened to her response, and added, "Yes, as soon as I can."

Mark hung up the phone. He looked first at his boss and then at the others. "My son is missing . . . downtown." He then glanced at his watch.

In a patronizing tone, the president concluded, "I'm sure your family and the authorities can handle the matter. Now, with a holiday tomorrow we've got a lot of ground to cover to make up for the lost time."

Mark, almost resigned to the situation, picked up his pointer, and turned back to the chart. His boss decided to rub it in. "I'd think you of all people, Mark, would understand the importance of putting first things first."

Mark slowly turned back to look at his employer, weighing what he had just said. He slowly placed his pointer on the table and glanced up at the company poster with its illustration of Scrooge. The miser seemed to scowl directly at Mark. Without further thought, Mark turned, snatched his jacket, gathered up his papers, and started to leave.

The president couldn't believe what he was seeing. Incredulously he demanded, "What do you think you're doing?"

Mark smiled kindly as he passed. "Why, I'm doing exactly

what you said to do, sir. I'm putting first things first."

Most of the executives seemed shocked. But it was all Karen could do to keep from laughing out loud.

Chapter 10

Christmas Eve had arrived far too soon for many shop-keepers. Surprisingly, the night and the storm had not dissuaded last-minute shoppers from making panicked purchases of unwanted gifts for undeserving relatives.

Shoppers passing by the bakery window watched as Gretchen Liesel took a tray of puffy white anise cookies from a cooling rack. She straightened a few and turned. She slid the tray into the window display and glanced up. Catching her breath, she reached out to touch her husband's arm as he passed. In a hushed voice, she exclaimed, "Look, Papa!"

The baker peered over his reading glasses. "What is . . . ? Ah, yes, I see."

David was framed in the bakery window, his wide eyes devouring the endless variety of pastries before him. The frost-tinged windowpane reflected a shimmering halo above his fine gold hair as his cheeks reddened from the cold.

Rolf and his wife stood transfixed by the moment. Gretchen's eyes filled at the emotion that swept over her. Almost to herself she whispered, "He looks like the cherub in the stained glass windows at the parish."

Her husband cleared his throat and then wiped his glasses. Reflectively, he said, "*Ja*, he does."

David glanced upward to see the pair watching him. Shyly, he smiled. At that moment, the little bell over the door demanded attention as customers entered the shop. A husband and wife entered, accompanied by a blast of arctic air and a little flurry of snow. David turned to leave while Rolf turned to greet the customers.

Gretchen held out her arms to the boy and converted the motion into a beckon, trying to coax the little boy into the warmth of the shop.

David looked back through the window and hesitated.

Gretchen snatched up a gingerbread angel cookie and rushed out the door, almost singing her greeting, "Merry Christmas!"

She stooped to David's height and extended the cookie by its sugarcoated wing. Shivering in the cold, her breath was visible.

David accepted the cookie with a shy smile, "Thank you." He took a bite and then turned to leave.

He's so small, Gretchen worried. She trembled again from the pervasive cold and called out to the boy as she motioned for him to come into the bakery. "It's so cold.

Won't you stay for a little while?"

The little boy only hesitated for a moment but shook his head. Eagerly, he called back, "It's almost Christmas, and I've got to find Jesus." David continued on his way. With a smile and a wave, he was gone.

Gretchen Liesel helplessly returned the wave. Her smile slowly faded into a look of deep concern. Then, reluctantly, she returned to the warmth of the bakery.

Mark slowly drove the family's 1939 Chevy coupe toward the toy store entrance. He fought for control on the slick roads. He looked for a parking spot, but then he spotted his sister-in-law through the snow-smeared windshield. Carefully, he pulled the car into the loading zone in front of the store. Caroline didn't wait for the car to stop. Instead, she ran to the passenger's side, yanked open the door, and jumped in. Mark's concern showed on his face. "Has anyone seen him?"

Caroline shook her head. "Not since he left the store," she responded in anguish. "He was right there with me in the toy store. He was watching the trains while I—" She looked out into the night. "I'm so sorry."

Mark reached across to reassure her. "Hey, Caroline, it's not your fault. He's a boy. You know how boys are." Then, offering assurances that Mark did not feel, he added, "He'll probably be back in a little while and tell us about some great adventure. We'll find him."

Caroline searched his face. Her expression tightened as she saw through his pretense. Mark was clearly more worried than he was letting on. Quietly she asked, "What do you want me to do?"

Mark glanced at his watch. Chewing his lower lip, he looked away so he wouldn't have to face her. "Uh, why don't you stay here in case he comes back? I'll start checking the shops down the road. If he comes back, or if I'm not back in an hour, go to our place and wait by the phone." Mark turned off the engine and gave her the house key from his key ring. He squeezed her arm reassuringly.

Caroline took the key, nodded grimly, and started to get out. "I've already called the police department. They said it was policy to wait twenty-four hours before they can do anything. I couldn't convince them this wasn't just another runaway. The dispatcher said she'd see what she could do. Maybe she'll put his description on the air . . . she's got a little boy."

Mark started the car. Impatiently, he looked over his shoulder. "I'll check back." Caroline stepped out into the snow and watched as Mark's car fought to get a grip on the road. The car's tires spun on the accumulated snow. Gaining traction, the car finally moved forward.

Chapter 11

B ob Slovak and two men struggled in the snow across the street from Slovak's police car. While they attempted to push a stuck motorist out of a snow bank, the unoccupied patrol car's radio crackled in the background. A loud beep sounded, and the police dispatcher came on the air. "All units . . . advisory . . . be on the lookout for a missing child. Male, Caucasian, approximately three feet ten inches tall . . . blond hair, blue eyes . . . last seen wearing a blue lightweight jacket, jeans, and sneakers. No other distinguishing . . . "

Slovak's face turned red, and his breath came in short bursts as the stuck car began to move. The radio blared in the background, but whatever he could distinguish over the sound of the spinning tires was buried by the sounds of the Salvation Army brass band on the far corner as they vigorously rendered a martial version of "Good King Wenceslas."

Slovak's offer of help was more than the extra efforts of a good public servant. The stranded car, a silver 1941 Chrysler Thunderbolt, was the car Bob coveted from the time he entered basic training during the war. It had been the dream for which he socked away most of his GI pay. The Thunderbolt's sleek body covered its white sidewall tires down to the middle of their hubcaps. Its straight lines and electric headlight covers made it look more like an aircraft than an automobile. It made all the other cars parked up and down the street look like antiques. Even though it was pre-war and over four years old, this car was the future as far as Bob was concerned. But now, with its steel chassis under hand, Slovak was forced to come to grips with the fact that this car was built like a tank. Even his considerable strength was proving useless in trying to free this behemoth.

Suddenly, the car moved forward, and Bob Slovak's legs were splattered with muddy snow. The spray moved up his uniform as the tires gained a grip the road. The driver of the newly liberated car leaned out the window and waved his thanks. "Thanks, you guys! Merry Christmas!"

The other two men waved back and went about their business as the silver car disappeared down the street. Bob Slovak just stared down at his muddy trousers. Disgusted, he stepped onto the curb and slapped at the muddy slush. Angrily, he muttered to himself, "Merry . . . Christmas! Pick pockets . . . shoplifters . . . drunks . . . family fights . . . not even a decent football game to listen to . . . ."

Slovak gave up on his uniform and looked around for any other motorists in trouble. Seeing none, he took a moment to look up at the snow falling from the sky. *It's going to be cold as h—* The thought fell incomplete, and he shivered involuntarily as his mind retreated back one year to what the war correspondents had called "the coldest, snowiest weather in memory."

In an instant, Bob was back in the Ardennes Forest on the German-Belgian border. The event had happened almost exactly one year ago, but for Bob Slovak, looking into the face of an oncoming storm was only one moment in time.

Slovak would turn twenty on January 6th. He'd lied about his age in late 1940. The army recruiter had no reason to doubt the tall, well-muscled kid who said he wanted to jump out of airplanes. If Bob had told the recruiting sergeant he was only fifteen, they would have sent him home, albeit reluctantly. Instead, he went to airborne training. When his mother learned what he had done, she was terrified. But she realized he'd been making the decisions of a man since his father died when Bob was only thirteen. She reluctantly held her peace.

The physical training, long runs, and endless push-ups were a snap for this oversized natural athlete. The tougher they made it, the more he enjoyed it.

Right out of jump school, Slovak was assigned to the 502nd parachute regiment, military police detachment. It was an assignment that would set the course for his post-war career.

In 1942, the 82nd Infantry Division was split in two, forming two new Airborne Infantry Divisions, the 82nd Airborne and the 101st Airborne. Both divisions had been stationed at Ft. Bragg, North Carolina, before being shipped overseas. North Carolina was okay, but Slovak couldn't wait to be reassigned. The training was monotonous, and Bob wanted to see the world. He wanted to fight.

In December 1943, Bob found himself in Belfast, Northern Ireland, where word reached him that his mother had passed away. Now he was alone. Christmas was coming, and there was no one with whom to share, no one to write, no one who cared. This was the beginning of his hatred for the season that up until now had always been his favorite. He refused to show any outward sign of his grief. He wouldn't even admit to himself how much he missed his mother. The letters, the knowledge she was there at home—those had been his anchors. Now he had no home but the army.

Bob relived that terrible Christmas Eve in 1944. Could it really have been just a year ago? The 501st Parachute Infantry Regiment and Company B of the Airborne Military Police Detachment had been ordered east toward Longvilly in an offensive move that had given the 101st time to secure their position. Snow fell, and the cold cut through the soldiers'

jackets like an ice-coated razor. Slovak's platoon was short of food and ammunition, and they lacked proper winter clothing. Most of the time they wrapped themselves in O.D. blankets in a vain attempt to keep warm.

Slovak occupied a secure position behind the stone railing of a small but strategic bridge that spanned a frozen creek. Snow and fog limited his visibility to about twenty-five yards. Big Bob hunkered down in his position, and his thoughts began drifting with the snow. Here he was, spending Christmas Eve hugging a cold stone bridge. His mom was gone, he was cold and hungry, and there were people out there who wanted to kill him. *What are you doing?* he asked himself angrily. *Stay alert and stop feeling sorry for yourself. There are people here depending on you.* He refocused on his field of fire.

The rest of the company was deployed in defensive positions on either side of the bridge. Slovak had recently been promoted to sergeant following a series of pitched battles that had decimated the company's NCO complement. He was now armed with a Thompson .45 caliber submachine gun.

In his mind's eye he could see the enemy patrol wearing GI uniforms, speaking perfect English. They even had the Abbot and Costello routine from their 1940s comedy, *One Night in the Tropics*, down pat. The "Who's on First?" routine always drew big laughs, but that night, it almost got Bob's unit killed.

Bob shuddered as he relived the vicious firefight that followed the discovery that they were Germans. His instincts
and quick reactions had saved the lives of the men in his
unit, but the battle had been vicious, and for Bob, it had cost
him what was left of his humanity.

"How in this God-forsaken war did you know, Slovak?"
his lieutenant had asked once the firefight was over.

Big Bob never did answer. He only remembered being
cold—colder than he'd ever been in his life. He stared at
his handiwork and said bitterly, "Merry Christmas." At that
moment, he knew he would never be the same.

Slovak forced himself to release the memories of combat
and stood shivering in the cold. In the distance, he could hear
the echoes of a department store loud speaker playing Bing
Crosby's recording of "Silent Night." It rang through the bitter
night air with an unearthly quality that deepened his feelings
of being alone in another place at a different time. He was still
in the process of shaking the memories of that Christmas past
when a small hand reached up and tugged twice on the side
of his great coat. Slovak whirled the wrong way and found no
one. Startled, he exclaimed, "What the—?"

Slovak looked over his other shoulder, but just as he did,
David had moved around to the man's other side. Once again,
Slovak found no one. Slovak pushed his service hat back,
scratched his forelock, and then shook his head, as if trying

to clear it. The small hand reached up again and yanked on the front of his coat. Startled, Slovak's head snapped down in disbelief.

Slovak found a tow-headed youngster, whose head was thrown back so he could look straight up at the towering officer. The boy showed his teeth in a forced smile that was almost a grimace. In a somewhat frightened voice, David stammered, "My . . . my mom said if I ever needed directions . . . or help . . . or anything . . . to ask a policeman." Slovak felt like a giant as he stood there glaring down at the boy—a giant who was having trouble maintaining his stern face.

Slovak took a step back. He was slightly annoyed. "A'right. A'right, kid. Whaddaya want?"

David was still looking up, but this new angle was easier on him. This giant standing before him frightened him, but his quest was more powerful than his fear. "Please, sir, will you tell me where I can find Jesus?"

Slovak was dumbfounded. Open-mouthed, he stared down at this Lilliputian who had suddenly commanded his attention. Then, slowly, the memories of war faded, and all the callousness drained from him. "Jesus, you say?"

Slovak looked around, smiled, and to no one in particular, said, "Okay. This morning I arrested Santa, and now I have a refugee from Charles Dickens on my hands." He looked down at the boy. "You're serious?"

David hunched his head down into his shoulders and

sheepishly smiled again as he nodded.

Slovak lowered himself into a crouch, bringing him nearly to David's height. *Sweet innocence of youth*, he thought as he took off his hat and vigorously massaged his rumpled hair. He considered the question for a moment and looked up as though trying to remember something.

"Well, now . . . if you were to walk two blocks down Jefferson—that's the next street over—you'll find a nativity scene in the parish courtyard. And there in the manger, next to his mother, you'll find the baby Jesus."

The little boy's face brightened. He immediately hurried off in the direction indicated, calling back over his shoulder, "Thanks, mister!"

Slovak stood slowly. Something that could almost pass for a smile cracked his somber expression. He called out, more to himself than to the boy, "My pleasure." Then, even more loudly, while shaking a finger he called, "See that you go straight home after, ya hear?"

Slovak watched the little boy disappear into the dark. There was no reply. Slovak stared after the boy for several seconds, and then he looked up at the snow, replaced his hat, and turned up his collar.

Chapter 12

Father Powell entered the parish dining room with his coat and muffler draped over his arm. He could barely see over his hat, which was perched precariously atop the stack of presents he carried. He sighed with resignation as he dumped the presents on the dining room table.

Mrs. Grogen, the parish housekeeper, came bustling in from the kitchen just as Father Powell knew she would. Her curly red hair was flecked with grey, a change that had done nothing, Father Powell noted, to soften her Irish temper. She carried a steaming cup of coffee and a plate on which rested a huge wedge of pie. Her expression was that of a mother insisting that her child eat his spinach.

Father Powell sighed heavily, dropped his coat and muffler on a chair, and straddled the one next to it. Mrs. Grogen firmly placed the pie, a fork, and a napkin in front of Father Powell, set the cup down next to it, and nodded with finality.

Father Powell took a huge bite of pie. With his mouth full, he mumbled, "There . . . see? I'm eating, I'm eating.' He took a swallow of coffee, reacted to its heat, and wiped his mouth. "Sometimes, Mrs. Grogen, I think you take such good care of me I'm in danger of being spoiled."

Mrs. Grogen gave the priest a knowing look. "No danger, Father, no danger a-tall. That happened a long time ago."

She gathered up her purse and dug out her keys. In a parental tone, she continued her lecture. "You'll be glad of the pie when you're out there in the cold, delivering gifts to the Johnson children." Then sweetly, she added, "And to your mother. Just leave the dishes. I'll clean up tomorrow afternoon after our family's Christmas brunch." Imperiously, she waved off any argument. "Mind you don't stay too long at your mother's. It'd be a scandal if you were late for midnight Mass."

Father Powell smiled sheepishly and nodded. "Thank you, Mrs. Grogen," he said. "Please give my best to your family. Will you lock the back door when you go out?"

Mrs. Grogen held up her keys and rattled them.

" 'Tis a shame it's necessary. But when vandals will steal the baby Jesus right out of the manger—"

Father Powell nodded sadly. "Took nearly a year to get it back. Sad to say, it's a different age. I'll lock the front." Warmly, he called out, "Merry Christmas, Mrs. Grogen!"

Mrs. Grogen exited with a wave. "Merry Christmas, Father," she called over her shoulder.

Father Powell came halfway out of his chair and craned his neck to make sure his housekeeper was gone. Satisfied, he shoved back the plate, hurried into his coat and muffler, grabbed the packages, and headed for the door.

The Nativity scene in the exterior courtyard was a tribute to the sculptor's art. Each life-sized figure had a character of its own. A shepherd stared toward the heavens directly into a brilliant blue-white light representing the star. His features, weathered from countless years tending flocks out in the open, reflected both fear and awe. A wise man, seated on his camel, also looked skyward. His richly appointed robes flowed outward, attesting to the haste with which he had undertaken his journey. His bearded features reflected excitement and wonder. The ox that knelt before the manger strained to see the wondrous event. An observer could almost feel the body heat of this placid beast. Joseph stood guard over his new family, his mature features set with concern and determination. He was dressed simply, but not poorly. Finally, a radiant teenage Mary peered into the manger. She had a timeless, classic beauty. Her expression was that of an adoring mother, but there was a hint of sadness on her otherwise serene features as she gazed down at her newborn.

A stained glass window, set directly above the crèche, cast an iridescent glow over all the figures. In its center was the figure of an angel, who looked remarkably like a little boy named David.

Suddenly, what appeared to be a shadow of a man crept up the wall next to the stained glass window.

Father Powell carefully locked the rectory door. He secured his muffler more snugly around his neck, shifted his packages more securely in his arms, and started down the walk. He had only taken a few steps when he noticed the shadow moving up the wall. He immediately stepped behind a column, caught his breath, and listened. He heard the crunch of footsteps in the snow, followed by the creak of a chain. Father Powell stepped out from behind the pillar just as the back-lit intruder was reaching out a hand toward the manger.

Father Powell dropped his packages and headed toward the trespasser at a dead run. He shouted angrily, "You there! Stop what you're doing!"

The intruder seemed torn between flight and reaching the crèche. Father Powell vaulted the restraining chain, grabbed the trespasser by the arm, and discovered that the intruder was nothing more than a small boy.

Surprised, he exclaimed, "Why, you're just a boy!" Father Powell leaned down for a closer look. He was scowling and, in the stark floodlights, he looked fierce.

David started trembling.

Father Powell demanded harshly, "What are you doing here?"

David was terrified and near tears. Almost too frightened

to respond, he said, "I . . . I'm just trying to find Jesus."

Father Powell straightened up, letting go of David's arm. "I see," said the priest, not seeing at all. "Well, you found him, but you mustn't touch. He's only to look at, you know."

David solemnly shook his head. His voice was heavy with disappointment. "That's just a doll. It's almost Christmas, and I have to find the *real* Jesus before it's too late."

Father Powell, far more kindly now but no longer interested in the boy, looked nervously at his watch. At the same time, he absently twisted and stroked his right eyebrow. In a detached manner, he started reclaiming his packages. "Nonsense . . . it's never too late." Father Powell inattentively reached out and patted David on the head. He was thinking of the tasks ahead and was in a hurry to leave. "But right now, I'm late for some important business. It's almost Christmas, you know. Come back tomorrow, bring your parents, and I'll tell you all about Jesus." Father Powell then turned on his heel and strode toward his car.

Through the tears running down his cheeks, David watched the priest leave. The distraught little boy turned and approached the manger. The doll representing the Christ Child was radiant. It seemed to reach up to the boy, its smile mature and knowing. David responded to the absent priest, "I already know about him. Mom and Dad told me he's our friend. But I have to find him . . . before it's too late."

David jammed his hands in his jacket pockets and

turned to leave. Although he was shivering with cold, he was determined. As David plodded down the street, he could hear the happy sounds of families and the music of Christmas coming from the warmly lit houses he passed by.

Chapter 13

Mark strained to see out of the windshield. The car's wipers were unable to keep up with the snow. He pounded his fist on the steering wheel in frustration. Finally, he saw a group of shops and pulled into the first available parking place. The sidewalk in front of the shops was filled to overflowing. Throngs of last-minute shoppers moved past shops, some entering as others were leaving. Mark exited the car and crossed the street, fighting his way through traffic and stepping up to the sidewalk. He glanced up at the sky and noted that the snowfall had increased. Mark was visibly worried now. He grabbed the first couple he encountered. They looked warily at him. Urgently, he asked, "Excuse me, have you seen a little boy, about this tall?" He held out his hand indicating his son's height. "He's blond with a light-weight blue jacket?"

The couple shook their heads and moved on. They turned

back to watch Mark over their shoulders as he stopped people along the way. Most seemed too busy to be bothered; others were nervous about being accosted by a stranger.

Soon he pleaded with those he stopped. "Please, have you seen a little boy about . . . this high? My little boy is missing."

Gretchen placed half a dozen marzipan cookies in a white box that already contained an assortment of strudel and anise cookies. She closed the lid, tied a string around it, and placed it on the counter by the window. She was printing the customer's name—S-T-E-W-A-R-T—on the box, when, through the window, she noticed Mark stopping passersby. He appeared worried as she watched him stop a teenager.

Gretchen moved to the window and, with a corner of her apron, cleared a spot so she could see more clearly.

"Papa!" she exclaimed. "Come see this!" The baker was busy wiping pans. He placed a pan on the rack and his towel on a hook, and moved to join his wife by the window.

Mark was standing by a distinguished-looking couple who were shaking their heads emphatically. As they moved out of the light from the bakery window, the woman clung to her husband's arm. They both looked back as though disturbed by Mark's questions.

The baker and his wife looked at each other. Gretchen was very concerned. "Papa, what is—?" Her husband shook his head slowly, as if trying to reason it out. "I don't know."

Gretchen's curiosity overcame her. She moved to the door, opened it just far enough to lean out, and called to Mark. "Can I help you?"

Mark rushed over to her. Frantically, he explained, "I'm looking for a little boy—my son. He's five . . . almost six . . . and he's lost."

The baker's wife was now deeply concerned. "Blond hair? Light blue jacket?"

Mark's face brightened with hope. Excitedly, he asked, "Where?"

Gretchen pointed down the street. "Sometime ago . . . He went down that way."

Mark took off running in the direction indicated. Gretchen called after him, "I gave him something to eat!" She re-entered the bakery. She turned to her husband and said with a hiss, "Such a terrible thing!"

Rolf was already putting on his coat and hat. He was a determined man. He turned to his wife and firmly commanded, "Close up, Mama! I'll get the car. We'll look around a little bit, *ja*? Put a note on the door . . . we'll be back in, oh, one hour." The baker turned toward the door. Gretchen grabbed a piece of paper and a marker and hastily wrote the note.

Mark now ran along the sidewalk with a hope born out of desperation. He slowed only to look in shop windows for some sign of his son. He was oblivious to the people he jostled along the way, but he left in his wake a trail of startled and angry faces. Some of the shops were closing.

Suddenly, Mark found himself caught in the beam of a brilliant spotlight.

Bob Slovak's voice was amplified by the patrol car's loud speaker. "Okay, mister, hold it right there!"

Mark stopped, staring back into the blinding light, holding his hand in front of his eyes in an attempt to see. The patrol car was just a vague shape behind the glare of the light.

Mark pleaded, "Please, I have to—"

Slovak's amplified voice was firmer now. "Step forward to the edge of the curb, please. Now, let's see both hands." It was not a request.

Mark complied. "Please . . . officer . . . ."

A shadow entered the circle of light, and a new, smaller beam of light hit Mark in the face. Slovak was back-lit by the patrol car spotlight. To Mark, he looked huge and ominous. He was holding a flashlight in his left hand, his right hand by his holster. "May I see some identification, please?" The "please" was a command.

Mark hurriedly fished his driver's license from his wallet. He shoved it toward the officer, impatient to be on his way. "Officer, if you'll just listen! My little boy is missing—he has been for several hours. He's not dressed for this weather."

Slovak snapped off his flashlight and handed back the driver's license. He listened, his face a granite mask—the only change was a slight tightening of the eyes when he heard the boy's description.

"He's just turning six . . . tomorrow's his birthday. He's blond . . . light blue jacket and jeans . . . too light for this storm. . . ."

Slovak, harshly, commanded, "Get in."

Mark desperately pleaded, "Please! I've got to find him!"

Slovak was already on his way back to the car. Insistent now, he barked, "Get in! I've seen him!"

Mark, with a new hope rising, rushed to the passenger side of the patrol car. The unit accelerated, the light bar flashed, and the car spun on its axis in the snow. No siren and very little sound could be heard. Inside the patrol car, Mark eagerly strained forward against the seat belt. "When did you see him?"

Slovak pursed his lips. "Maybe half an hour, forty-five minutes ago . . . ."

When an oncoming vehicle failed to stop in time for the police car, the driver panicked and succeeded only in sliding, rear end first, in their direction.

Slovak reacted angrily. "You jerk!" He skillfully avoided a collision and then shook his fist at the hapless driver of the other car. Slovak was fuming. He rolled down his window and shouted, "Did you fall asleep behind the wheel?" He gestured to the flashing lights of the patrol car. "What do you think these are? Christmas tree lights?"

Mark was shaken.

Slovak, now under control and moving forward down the road, told him, "Your boy asked for directions to the parish.

Mark, incredulous, responded, "What?"

Slovak nodded. "Darnedest thing I ever saw. He looked like he'd just stepped out of a Christmas card or something."

Mark was trying to understand. "But we're not Catholic."

Slovak shrugged.

Chapter 14

A street vendor, dressed in a Dickens-period costume, warmed his hands over a glowing barrel. He was selling roasted chestnuts from a 55-gallon drum that he had rigged into a charcoal grill. The police car, its lights still flashing, turned the corner at the far end of the block.

David was huddled behind the drum trying to get warm and, from that position, he was unseen by the searchers. A vendor beckoned to passersby to come buy his wares. He wore a tall hat, a long black-frocked coat, and mutton chop sideburns. He sang his sales pitch in a loud, rich baritone voice. "Chestnuts, roasted Chestnuts . . . No better way to beat the cold . . . Try my chestnuts . . . They're hot and they're good . . . They'll warm you right down to your toes!" The vendor used tongs to place several piping hot chestnuts in a paper cup. He handed the cup to David and gave him a big wink.

David smiled up at him.

The baker and his wife searched intently as they drove slowly down the street. Their concern grew with each passing moment. Gretchen scanned the sidewalk on her side of the car. She saw the vendor and the makeshift charcoal grill, but David remained hidden from her view.

The street vendor busily scooped chestnuts into small paper sacks and handed them to customers. He sang as he made change. "Chestnuts! Get your hot, sweet chestnuts!"

Slovak pulled the police car to a stop in front of the parish. Mark exited and hurried up the walk. Bob Slovak stood in the background by the open door on the driver's side. He played the spotlight around the building, finally stopping at partially covered footprints in the snow. Mark pounded on the parish door. At first, he hammered vigorously, pausing to put his ear to the door to detect any response. Then he hit the door with slow, measured blows of anger and frustration. Finally, he leaned against the door in defeat. To himself he pleaded, "Where—?"

Slovak quietly observed, "He's been here."

Mark raced down the sidewalk to join Slovak, who stood near the manger scene. The big cop pointed his flashlight on the snow, examining some depressions in the snow with professional detachment. Mark moved to his side. Slovak used his flashlight as a pointer to illustrate what he had deduced.

Slovak narrated matter-of-factly, as though he was dictating a crime scene report. "He was here . . . maybe half an hour ago. Looks like someone came over to him from over there." He moved the beam of light to the spot where Father Powell had been standing, "Then he left—alone."

Mark looked at Slovak quizzically. "How do you know?"

Slovak pointed out some distant tracks with his flashlight. He responded with professional detachment. "The tracks are almost covered, but you can make out the depressions. One small set of tracks coming in from the direction of town." Slovak then swung his light toward the parish door. "A big set coming from the parish. They meet here. Whoever came out that door had to have seen the boy. The depth of snow coverage is almost identical."

Deeply worried, David's Dad tried to be patient. "And . . . ? Where are they?"

"Not they." Indicating with his flashlight, Slovak continued, "The large tracks lead that way, where a car was parked. See where it blocked the snow? The small tracks lead the other way, back toward town—alone."

Caroline stood with the telephone in hand. She paced

back and forth like a caged animal. Every few steps, she brushed ineffectually at the drooping curl on her forehead. Suddenly, the waiting became too much for her to withstand. She froze, gripped the phone with both hands, and dialed a number that, by then, had become indelibly imprinted in her memory.

"Police dispatch, may I help you?"

"Yes, please! Is there anything new on my missing nephew?"

The police dispatcher, who was on the line talking to Caroline, reached for another call report form. A sprig of pine with a tartan bow and a tiny red tree ornament had been taped to the console. Christmas spirit was sparse at headquarters. In the background, other dispatchers handled the steady, incoming stream of calls in the order received. The police dispatcher remained patient and professional as she took Caroline's call.

"Your name, ma'am? And the child's name, please?" She carefully checked her notes before responding, "No, ma'am, nothing new . . . we'll call you . . . give me that number then . . . of course; you'll be called at your home the moment we have anything to report. Yes, ma'am. It's standard procedure."

Caroline hung up the phone and resumed pacing. She opened the refrigerator, stared blankly at its contents, and then closed the door without removing anything. She walked to the sink, turned on the water, and filled a glass that overflowed without her noticing. Absentmindedly, she left the glass on the counter without taking a drink. She then resumed her restless pacing.

Bob Slovak and Mark continued to drive through the streets. They searched diligently, but their mood was somber. Mark deliberated out loud, more to himself than to Slovak, "It's the little things that are the hardest. Sometimes I'll find a note she left that I'd missed . . . she used to do that . . . leave little notes for me to find. Nothing important . . . 'Don't forget to take this suit to the cleaners' or 'Even here in the sock drawer, you'll find that I love you—even if I didn't mend your socks.' " He turned to Slovak. "She hated mending." Slovak stared straight ahead, but he was both moved and troubled by the other man's grief.

"Just last week, I found a note in the pocket of a jacket I haven't worn since last year. It said, 'I can hardly wait for you to walk through the door each night. Come give me a hug and tell me that you love—' " He turned to look out the window, tears welling in spite of his resolve. "I just sat there in the middle of the floor, crying like a little kid. If it hadn't been for our son, I don't think I'd have made it."

Slovak shifted uncomfortably. He hesitated for a moment, reluctant to speak. "Does he know how you feel?"

Mark was taken aback, "What? Who?"

Slovak responded with professional reserve. "Your son.

Does he know how you feel about him?"

Mark was instantly defensive. "Why, yes . . . of course he does!"

Slovak just nodded, concentrating on the street.

Mark studied the big cop, trying to see through his stony exterior. "Why do you ask?"

Slovak shrugged. He thought for a moment before answering. Then, in a frank, matter-of-fact tone, he said, "Your little boy is lost out there in the snow. The storm is building—the temperature's dropping—and you're talking about your dead wife. I know you care about your son . . . I just wondered if your son knows how much you care."

Mark was stunned. At first, he started to protest, but Slovak's words cut him deeply. He looked back out the window. Introspectively, he tried to convince himself. "He knows . . . he must know. He's . . . my whole life. We do things together. We talk . . . sometimes." There was a long pause, and then Mark groaned, "Oh, no! . . . He wanted to talk about his mother this morning, and I just put him off." Then, after another long pause, "Oh, how could I have been so stupid?"

Slovak had become even more uncomfortable. Somewhat apologetically, he tried to soften his criticism. "Look, I'm just a cop. I ask questions for a living. Don't take anything I say personally."

Mark was now deeply troubled about more than David's disappearance. He shifted uncomfortably. Then, deeply grieved, he demanded, "Look . . . I've got to do something! Please take me back to my car. I can't just sit here while he's out there."

Slovak scowled out the windshield. He tried to change Mark's mind.

"Look, I'll do what you want, but I think you're making a mistake. Two sets of eyes are less likely to miss him. Besides, the dispatcher will notify us if there's any word. And I'm not so sure you should be driving around in the snow by yourself."

Chapter 15

Joshua sat partway up a set of stairs, just out of the snow. He sat with his head resting on his hands, watching the parade of last minute shoppers passing by below him. He had a keen mind and wisdom beyond his age. Virtually nothing escaped his scrutiny.

He sat on the stairs, not because he had nothing to do, but because one of his favorite games was to see what he could discover about the individuals in the parade below. He had learned, even in his tender years, that people revealed themselves just by the way they dressed, walked, and carried themselves. And, most of all, he had learned that they tended to reveal their true character by the way they interacted with others.

He was far more than a gifted black child. He was a favored and treasured member of his community. Everyone who met him came away astonished by his matter-of-fact grasp of the world around him. The universal assessment of those who met him was that he was a future leader. In a letter, his daddy had written to his mother, he had called Joshua "my little old man—six going on sixty."

Joshua looked back over his shoulder in response to the sounds of Christmas carols being sung by a choir—an exceptionally gifted choir—just inside the upstairs door. Joshua leaned forward as something caught his interest. He tilted his head slightly and strained to see.

On the street below, Joshua watched a small boy stopping people as they passed by. This was something new, and his curiosity was piqued. He couldn't hear what the other boy was asking, but people's reactions were strikingly varied, and that, more than anything else, was what had captured Joshua's attention.

He first noticed the boy when he tugged at the sleeve of a well-dressed man. The man stopped and leaned over, keeping his body as far from the boy as possible. The man listened for a second and then waved his hand at the sky and walked on.

What's that about? Joshua wondered. He moved down a couple of steps for a better view. The boy Joshua was watching walked back and forth for a moment. He approached a middle-aged woman holding a shopping bag in one hand. She listened to the boy for a second and then turned and pointed up toward the sky.

Joshua rested his chin on his hand and watched intently,

trying to figure out what the other boy was doing. The boy in the blue jacket walked slowly up the street.

Joshua watched the older people intently as they passed. *He's searching for a friendly face,* Joshua surmised.

The boy finally approached two women walking together. The first woman patted him on the head and turned to the other. They walked on without stopping. *They're treating that boy like he's some kinda puppy dog,* Joshua thought in disgust.

David stopped on the street below. Discouraged, his shoulders sagged. The flow of humanity broke around him as if he was a rock in a stream. Then he saw a Salvation Army worker ringing a bell by a kettle. David asked him a question. The man responded, without breaking the rhythm of his bell, by placing his left hand over his heart. David shook his head and walked on. His path led him ever closer to Joshua's vantage point.

Joshua canted his head and scowled. Joshua was visible from the street, but David was totally unaware that he was being watched. Joshua continued to watch intently as David approached a minister. *That's good,* Joshua thought. But then the man's expression and body language suggested he was somewhat condescending. Joshua scowled again as the minister seemed to listen to the boy's question, straighten up, and spread his hands in a sweeping motion toward the sky.

Joshua moved partway down the stairs. He leaned over the rail and watched this strange scene with unabashed curiosity.

The poor little boy seemed desperate now. He tried to stop several people who totally ignored him. Then he succeeded in stopping three teenagers. The leader of the pack leaned back as he listened to the boy's question. Then he stuck his nose in David's face and wagged his head from side to side derisively. Then the three teenagers swaggered on, laughing and punching each other in the upper arm in congratulations at the apparent joke.

Joshua's curiosity had taken control of him. He moved a couple of steps further down the stairs.

David had now reached a point opposite the foot of the steps. He appeared very discouraged.

Joshua called out to him in friendly tones, "Hey, boy!"

David stopped and looked around for the source of the voice.

Joshua then asked, "Whatcha doin'?"

David tried to smile but failed. "I'm trying to find Jesus."

Joshua's head snapped back in surprise and his eyes grew large. Astonished, he asked, "Why you doin' that?"

In desperation, David replied, "Tomorrow's Christmas, and by then it'll be too late. Do you know where I can find him?"

Joshua was totally taken aback by the response. He thought for a moment, shook his head solemnly, and then he brightened as if something had occurred to him. He smiled excitedly and offered, "But I bet my mama does!" He motioned for David to follow him and turned up the stairs.

On the door at the head of the stairs, in neat, gold letters, was the legend, "Grace Baptist Church." Joshua opened the door and motioned for his new friend to hurry. The choir music was noticeably louder with the door open.

Just as the church door closed behind the boys, Bob Slovak and Mark passed slowly in front of the church building. Both men stared intently out their respective windows.

Inside Grace Baptist Church, the choir ended the number it had been rehearsing. The choir director, Charles Biggs, looked at his notes. Biggs was the owner of the local record shop. Music was his life. His collection of jazz recordings was one of the most complete in the nation. It had everything from W. C. Handy's "St. Louis Blues" and the original 1931 Hoggy Carmichael recording of "Rockin' Chair" to Andy Preer and the Cotton Club Orchestra's rendition of "I've Found A New Baby," recorded just before Preer's death in 1927. But Biggs's greatest love was choir music. His taste was eclectic to say the least. He coveted and collected everything from the Vienna Boy's Choir to the Mormon Tabernacle Choir. If it was gospel music, he lived it and loved it.

"That was beautiful, people!" Biggs exclaimed. "Tomorrow will be the finest Christmas program we've ever had. Now, let's rehearse the solo. Where's our star?" He looked around expectantly.

Joshua's mother stepped down from her position in the choir and came over to the boys. She looked at the two questioningly. "Joshua? Why aren't you ready? This is a dress rehearsal. Come on, child." She reached out her hand to her son.

Joshua's mother, Mary Beth, was a well-educated and highly respected member of the neighborhood. As a high school librarian, she had helped set standards of excellence for the students in her community. As the wife of a career Air Force fighter pilot, she and her son had endured long months of separation from their husband and father. But they were proud of his ground-breaking achievements. He was one of the leaders of the highly decorated Tuskegee Airmen, who not only contributed to the successful conclusion of the war in Europe, but who had also broken down barriers and garnered new respect and acceptance for Americans of African descent in the military. He was a hero to his family, of course, but he had become a national hero as well. No bomber, under escort by fighters from his command, had ever been lost to enemy fighters. The red-tailed P-51 Mustangs flown by the Tuskegee Airmen symbolized security to all bomber crews and a talisman for victory throughout the European theater.

Joshua looked at David and shrugged. He moved to the front bench where his robe had been folded neatly over the backrest. Joshua smiled sheepishly at David as his mother helped him on with his choir robe and adjusted it carefully.

She spoke quietly and privately to her son. "Now, Joshua, you know that everybody in the congregation loves you. They love to hear you sing. So you just forget about everything, but letting the Lord know how much you love him. . . . All right?"

Joshua nodded slightly. Then, glancing over at the unknown boy, his mother asked, "Who's your friend?"

Joshua scrunched his shoulders in an "I don't know" kind of shrug. "He says he's trying to find Jesus. I told him you know all about him."

Joshua's mother raised her eyebrows in surprise and pleasure. She walked over and gave David a big, loving bear hug. Then, warmly, she greeted her son's new friend. "Hello. I'm Joshua's mama, and I understand you're trying to find my best friend. You sit down right here and as soon as we finish singing, I'll tell you all about him."

David nodded and then craned his neck to see what Joshua was doing. Joshua had taken his place on a wooden box just to the side of the choir. The box was decorated with cloth drapes in the choir's colors. At first, Joshua seemed self-conscious as he fidgeted with his robe, but as the music started playing, his face softened, and he was soon lost in the music.

Biggs began leading with small strokes, close to his chest, which indicated a very soft introduction. The piano player began the prelude to "O Holy Night." His was not a typical rendition; the introduction was rich and full. It was soon apparent that the accompanist's talent was worthy of any concert stage. His eyes were closed as he moved with the music, which he seemed to feel in the depth of his soul.

At a "come to me" gesture from Biggs, the choir added its harmonic breath to the prelude. They too were gifted musicians who understood how to probe the depth of human emotion.

The choir director turned to Joshua and smiling widely, he reached out with a motion that suggested he was drawing Joshua to him. The young boy lifted his chin and sang with a voice that rang through the hall like a bell. His crystal clear voice filled the room.

> O holy night, the stars are brightly shining;
> It is the night of the dear Savior's birth.

David sat up in surprise. He was entranced by this new friend's singing. He moved so that he could get a better view and rested his chin on both hands while Joshua was totally absorbed in the music:

> Long lay the world in sin and error pining,
> 'Til he appeared and the soul felt his worth.

Joshua's mother had returned to her place in the choir. Her eyes glistened as the twin emotions of love and pride overflowed. Her son's voice filled the night.

> A thrill of hope, the weary world rejoices;
> For yonder breaks, a new and glorious morn.

The choir was remarkable. They sang as a unit, polished and professional. Their balanced harmonies overflowed the room and moved through the snowy night beyond.

> Fall on your knees! O, hear the angel voices!
> O night divine; o night when Christ was born.

Even Biggs's eyes were now closed in adoration. The choir joined in the exultation:

> O night divine; o night, o night divine.

The pianist then performed a stirring interlude. The voices of the choir supplied the orchestration, some sounding remarkably like the instruments they imitated.

On the street below, Bob Slovak had pulled over to the snow-covered curb and Mark exited the patrol car. The music from upstairs carried down onto the street below, but Mark was too focused on his quest to notice. He leaned in the open door. "I hope I'm right. It just seems to me that if we're both looking, we've got a better chance. I know if I just sat there any longer, I'd go over the edge." He slammed the door and stepped back as the police car started to move. As an afterthought, he called out, "I don't know how to . . . . Thanks! Thanks a lot!"

Slovak brushed aside the thanks and pulled away.

Mark rushed to his car, which was already nearly buried under newly fallen snow. He glanced around, noting that most of the stores had closed and that the sidewalks were virtually empty. He used his arm to clear the windshield and was about to enter the car when he heard the angelic tones of a small boy sing the third verse of "O Holy Night" drifting down to the street, stopping Mark in his tracks. He turned toward the source.

> Truly he taught us to love one another;
> His law is love and his gospel is peace.

Mark closed his eyes in pain. He listened for a moment and then uttered a desperate prayer. "Please, Lord, help me find him—before it's too late." He then entered his car, backed up and drove away on the nearly empty streets.

Joshua's solo voiced truths that he was too young to fully understand.

> Chains shall he break for the slave is our brother;
> And in his name all oppression shall cease.

The director conducted with minimal movements now, as he watched Joshua with something closely akin to awe. David listened as though he had never heard music before.

> Sweet hymns of joy in grateful chorus, raise we;
> Let all within us praise his holy name.

The choir moved into the finale. They were not just a collection of gifted singers; they were a unified instrument of humanity—a finely tuned ensemble that breathed and sounded as one.

Christ is the Lord; Him ever praise we!

Then, Joshua sang his final solo phrase.

His power and glory; ever more proclaim.

David, from his position in the back of the hall, looked at the choir and was reminded of the Christmas card his family had sent to family and friends the year before.

Joshua and choir now united.

His power and glory; ever more proclaim!

Everyone froze for a moment. The entire structure seemed to ring with the final note. At first, no one wanted to break the magic of the moment. Then, the director turned toward Joshua and raised his hands. The entire choir broke into vigorous applause.

Joshua was surprised and then embarrassed. He ran over to his mother. She picked him up and gave him a big squeeze. "I am so proud of you, Joshua!" She put him down, and he immediately dragged her over to where David was waiting.

She looked at the boy with renewed interest and asked, "Did you enjoy the music?"

David smiled shyly and nodded. Several members of the choir gathered around. Joshua's friend was a bit of a curiosity. The choir had a number of admirers among the white community, but an unattended blond child had piqued the interest of many in the group. One of them was the choir's basso profundo. Even his speaking voice was spectacular.

"Hey, Joshua, you were fantastic! Who's your friend?"

Joshua looked at David matter-of-factly. "He's trying to find Jesus." The group reacted with a mixture of surprise and satisfaction.

The bass stooped to the boy's height. "Well, you're certainly in the right place."

Joshua's mother asked gently, "Tell us, boy, what do you already know about Jesus?"

David thought for a moment. Then, he politely responded, "Mom and Dad told me he's Heavenly Father's son." The group gathered around David smiled in agreement. David continued, "They also told me he's our friend, and he loves us." More choir members crowded around the boy. They were deeply touched.

"And he made it possible for us to go back to heaven someday."

The bass responded quietly, and sincerely. "Your people taught you well, boy."

Joshua turned to his mother and tugged on her sleeve. Eagerly, he said, "Now, you tell him, Mama, you tell him."

His mother chuckled, shaking her head at her son's enthusiasm. "And just where do you think I should start?"

Joshua clapped his hands in excitement. "Mary's Boy Child, Mary's Boy Child!"

Joshua's mother was amused by her son's eagerness. "Why, that's the very place!" She smiled at the boys, folded her hands in her lap, and looked up at the ceiling as if remembering that day so long ago. Her song was a cross between spiritual and calypso. Her voice was mellow and full. It stirred the soul.

> Long time ago, in Bethlehem, So the Holy Bible say,
> Mary's boy child Jesus was born on Christmas day.

Members of the choir spontaneously added rich harmony. Other choir members, who had been about to leave, paused, hung their coats over the back of the nearest pew, and returned to join in the song. Mary Beth and the choir members joined together in singing the chorus.

> Hark, now hear the Angels sing, new King's born today.
> And man shall live forevermore, Because of Christmas day.

Joshua's mother turned to David and seemed to be singing just to him.

> While shepherds watched their flocks by night,
> They saw a bright, new shining star.

Joshua moved to David's side and rested his hand on David's shoulder.

> And heard a choir from heaven sing . . .
> The music came from afar.

As she ended the verse, she prompted Joshua to sing

the chorus. He copied his mother's style. As he sang, David watched intently.

> Hark; now hear the Angels sing,
> New King's born today.

When the choir members joined in, David sang with them—much to the amusement of everyone in the room.

> And man will live forevermore,
> Because of Christmas day.

Now the bass took the lead, and it was clear that the other choir members admired him. The rest of the choir hummed the harmony as his deep, rich voice filled everyone's hearts.

> Now, Joseph and his wife, Mary, came to Bethlehem that
>   night.
> They found no place to bear her child; Not a single room was
>   in sight.

The rest of the choir hummed a musical bridge that changed the key. During the bridge, Joshua's mother moved over to David and took both of his hands in hers. She was now singing just for him. The mood of the final verse was more personal, more reverent.

> By and by, they found a little nook in a stable all forlorn.
> And in a manger, cold and dark, Mary's little boy child was
>   born.

The choir members joined the final chorus. They put everything they had into their song, as though they were proclaiming the event to the whole world.

> Trumpets sound and Angels sing, Listen to what they say.
> That man will live forevermore because of Christmas day.

After the song, several choir members glanced at their watches and headed for the door. They waved at the rest who gathered around David.

" 'Night!"

"Merry Christmas!"

"Drive careful, ya hear?"

"See you early tomorrow!"

"Merry Christmas!"

Joshua's mother stood in front of the boys. The remaining choir members were immediately behind her. Smiling she asked, "Now then, do you have any questions?"

David zipped up his coat, getting ready to leave. He nodded. His eyes were filled with tears. "Where can I find Jesus? I have to go see him. It's almost Christmas, and by then it'll be too late."

Mary Beth's smile faded. It was replaced by a look of concern. She looked at her fellow choir members for help.

The bass extended his hand. "Hi, I'm Don." He shook his head slowly. "Son, that's a hard question to answer. Outside of heaven, the only thing that comes to mind is . . . well, the Bible says that when the prophets wanted to talk to the Lord face to face, they got themselves up to a high mountain."

David tried to grasp what the man said, and then his face lit up. For the first time in his quest, David felt real hope, and he ran for the door.

The remaining choir members looked at each other in bewilderment. Joshua called after him. "Hey, where you going?"

David disappeared through the open door. A flurry of snow blew in, followed by silence.

Chapter 16

A weary Bob Slovak stood in the police station locker room. In the process of changing into his civvies, the gnawing ache in his gut grew worse. He reached into his locker, took out a heavy parka, and jammed his arms into it.

Three lockers to his right, Rick Franklin, the station practical joker, was just coming on duty. Franklin was one of those rare and obnoxious individuals who didn't care what others thought of him. His ruddy face wore a perpetual sneer as he swaggered his way through life. He'd only managed to survive in the company of other members of the force because of his size—and the fact that he spent much of his spare time lifting weights. Franklin slammed his locker shut, picked up his clipboard and flashlight, and made his way past Slovak and several of the other officers present. Franklin looked straight ahead as he deliberately knocked Charlie Cooper's hat off the bench, trying to make it look like an accident.

Charlie reacted with disgust. "Grow up, Franklin!"

Franklin raised both eyebrows in mock surprise. "Touchy, touchy! You're just sore because I won the football pool."

Charlie waved him off with loathing. Franklin moved on and stopped, hovering over Slovak for a moment. "Well, Slovak, I suppose you've got a hot date to some Christmas party while we married guardians of the peace toil through the night."

Slovak gathered his personal belongings and his flashlight. "Nope, I'm going out to help look for that missing kid."

Franklin looked incredulous. "You're kidding!" He turned to the others still in the locker room. "Hey, guys, listen up! Scrooge here has gone and got the Christmas spirit." He patted Slovak on the shoulder in mock camaraderie.

Slovak clenched his jaw, looked up at the hulking patrolman, and then, in a move so fast that Franklin had no time to react, Slovak grabbed Franklin's wrist and effortlessly forced him to his knees. It was a submission hold he had used many times in the military. Through clenched teeth he snarled, "Knock it off, Franklin! I saw the kid. I talked to him. I could have reached out and grabbed him. Instead I sent him off. He's still out there somewhere. I spent the last part of my patrol driving the kid's father around, listening to him talk about the family he used to have."

Slovak let Franklin go, turned, and slammed his locker shut. Franklin got up and stood there awkwardly. Unable to say a word, he looked down at his shoes.

Chapter 17

Father Powell stood patiently beside his car, while the lot attendant and one of the Boy Scouts working in the Christmas tree lot finished tying a tree to the roof of his car. A small family carefully examined the remaining trees. The kids wanted the biggest tree they could find, but their parents, assisted by other scouts, carefully selected a much more modest specimen.

The attendant finished lashing down Father Powell's selection, went over to the sales shed, and returned with a large sack. Father Powell reached for his wallet. The attendant shook his head firmly. "Put that away, Father! Do you want to deprive me of some blessings?"

Father Powell smiled broadly. "I'd never want to do that, Michael."

The lot attendant looked closer at the priest. "How is it you remember my name, Father? I'm not Catholic."

"Well," Father Powell replied, his breath visible in the cold night air, "you could chalk it up to the fact that St. Michael is my patron saint . . . or, the fact that year after year, I come here to buy a tree for a poor family, and you never let me pay. But the fact is, you're a thoroughly good man, Michael. There are precious few thoroughly good men in this world. I treasure those that I find, no matter what their faith. Besides, there aren't many Mormon bishops in these parts, and I've heard about all the work you've done for the members of your congregation and their needy neighbors. Yes, Michael, I know who you are, and I'd like to call you 'friend.' "

Bishop Michael Tanner was moved. He took off his glove and extended his hand. Father Powell responded in kind.

"I'd be honored, Father Powell."

Now, Father Powell was somewhat surprised. "How is it you recall my name, you not being Catholic and all?"

Michael smiled at the priest. "Well, you could chalk it up to the fact that Powell is my grandmother's maiden name . . . or, the fact that year after year, you come here to get a tree for a poor family. But the fact is, you have a reputation for going out of your way to help people, regardless of their religion. I admire that. I'm proud to have you as a friend."

Michael handed Father Powell the sack he had been holding. "Here's a stand, a couple of small strings of lights, and some tinsel. Maybe it'll help bring the spirit of Christmas to someone who needs it. I just wish I could come with you. Playing Santa's helper—now, that's what's Christmas is all about. But I've been out of touch too long as it is, and I suspect there are a number of families who will need my help as soon as I get home."

Father Powell looked at the sky and grinned. "I'll admit it, Bishop. I look forward to this all year. I can hardly wait for it to get dark . . . it makes me feel like a kid again. Maybe one year you and your family will join me. It's a great adventure, and there are so many families who need help. Lord bless you, Michael."

Michael responded soberly, "He does, Father, he does. Merry Christmas!"

Father Powell drove off the lot with a wave. He turned on the radio, filling the car with Christmas carols. The current carol ended, and the announcer read his station break. "You are listening to 'The Sounds of Christmas' on AM-1220. Current temperature is 26 degrees. Due to heavy snowfall in the valley, the highway patrol urges you to stay off the roads if at all possible. Up to two feet of snow is expected over the next few hours."

At the radio station, Kelly Green sat at the microphone. Several empty Pepsi bottles had been stacked in an artistic pyramid on the table next to the console. Kelly continued the weather report. "The storm is expected to last until midnight, leaving us with clear skies and temperatures dropping below zero. So, throw another log on the fire and enjoy 'The

Sounds of Christmas' on AM-1220."

Kelly punched the button for the next series of Christmas carols, shut off his mike, and let out a long, audible sigh. He took a final pull on his Pepsi, crumpled a sheet of paper into a ball, and made an exaggerated hook shot into the waste can. He then got up and added the empty Pepsi bottle to the growing pyramid.

Father Powell turned onto a quiet street in a poor section of town as the Christmas music resumed. As he drove, something troubled him. In his mind, he heard the echoes of a statement made by the young boy he had seized at the church's manger scene. "That's just a doll. . . . It's almost Christmas, and I have to find the *real* Jesus before it's too late."

Father Powell frowned. Just then, he saw his destination and the thought was forgotten. He exited the car and walked carefully to a side window of a rather simple house. Father Powell looked around to make sure he hadn't been seen.

He was unaware that a nosy next-door neighbor stood behind her drapes, watching him as he peeked in the window.

The meddlesome woman was dressed in a stained robe and ragged slippers. Her hair was in curlers and her makeup was caked and smeared. She had a can of beer in one hand and a feisty mop-of-a-dog in the other. Both her disposition and the dog's temperament left a great deal to be desired.

Through the window, Father Powell could see the objects of his stealthy visit. In the sparsely furnished living room was a widow and her three small children. The little ones were all in their pajamas, which were clearly too small for them. Seated on a well-worn couch, their faces beamed in anticipation of the magical day to come. The widow's attempt at holiday cheer was transparent. A bowl of popcorn and three apples sat on the table. Small presents were nearby, all gift-wrapped without bows. Their shape suggested either pajamas or other small items of clothing. The rest of the house was neat and tidy but obviously furnished with hand-me-downs.

Father Powell was suddenly startled by a raspy voice and the yapping of a tiny dog behind him. The snooping crone from next-door leaned out on her porch and demanded belligerently, "Who the devil're you, and whaddaya doing peeping in that window?"

Father Powell checked the window to make sure he hadn't been discovered. He then put his finger to his lips and approached the nosy neighbor on exaggerated tiptoe. He gave her an impish grin.

In an exaggerated stage whisper, he commanded, "Hush now! I'm Saint Nicholas, and if you give me any trouble, I'll tell my elves down at City Hall that you don't have a vicious animal permit for that beast!"

The slightly intoxicated neighbor beat a hasty and

indignant retreat, slamming the door behind her. Father Powell muttered to himself as he went back to his car. "Lord, give me strength." He removed the tree from the top of his car and grabbed the packages and sack of decorations. Quietly, he made his way to the front porch of the house. With great care, he propped the tree in a corner where it would be seen. He then placed the presents in front of the door and returned to his car.

The slovenly neighbor and her dog watched from inside their house. She turned to her canine companion and in a slurred, voice she observed, "St. Nick, my great aunt's knickers!"

Father Powell took several bags of groceries out of his trunk. Quietly, he returned to the porch and placed the groceries next to the gifts. He dug into the pocket of his overcoat and came out with a large red bow, which he affixed to the groceries. He then probed the other pocket of his greatcoat and pulled out a leather strap studded with large sleigh bells. Father Powell looked around carefully, picked his hiding place, and then took a deep breath.

Shaking the sleigh bells for all he was worth, Father Powell stomped on the porch, making as much noise as possible. "Ho! Ho! Ho! Merry Christmas, everybody! Merry Christmas!"

Father Powell heard squeals of excitement from the children inside the house. He rang the doorbell and took off running. He made it behind a bush just as the door burst open and a gaggle of excited children emerged. Out of breath, Father Powell chuckled to himself. "I'm getting too old for this!"

He watched from his hiding place as the children jumped up and down with excitement. They carried the tree and all of the packages inside until only the widow was left on the porch. She stood for a moment looking about. Her eyes glistened. With tender emotion, she called out into the night, "Thank you! And God bless you, whoever you are."

Father Powell waited for several minutes before returning to his car. He sat behind the wheel for a time, savoring the moment. "That felt good. That felt very good!"

Chapter 18

Mark waited impatiently inside the hospital emergency room receiving area. He pounded one gloved fist into the other gloved hand as he waited for the receptionist to check on the latest admissions. He found it increasingly difficult to stand still. He began to pace like a feral animal in a cage. He moved to the double-glass doors to check on his car, which he had left idling in front of the entrance.

A security officer entered through the double doors and, seeing Mark peering out, asked, "Is that your car, sir?"

Mark turned to him impatiently. "Yes, officer, it is. I'll just be a minute. This is an emergency."

The security officer had heard this excuse too many times. "Yes, sir, they all are. You'll have to move it."

Mark turned away and looked impatiently at a nurse on the phone in the back office. He played for time. "Okay . . . I'll be right there."

The security officer shook his head and exited through the double doors. Mark looked around the stark reception area.

To Mark, the hospital was a terrible place that brought back memories still too vivid and painful. In his mind, he could hear the echoes of the doctor's voice as he shattered Mark's dreams for the future. "I'm sorry. It's progressed too far. There's nothing we can do for her . . . nothing we can do . . . nothing . . . "

From behind him, the nurse echoed his memories. "I'm sorry, sir. There's nothing we can do."

Mark was startled back to reality. He turned to the nurse who had been on the phone. Standing just across the reception desk, the nurse was clearly concerned. "I've checked with admitting and pediatrics. I'm sorry. No little boy matching your description has been admitted."

Mark mumbled his thanks and was on his way out the door. "Where could he be?" he asked himself—and God. Mark slammed through the double doors toward his idling car. The security officer from before was moving to the back of Mark's car. He had his ticket book out and was just reaching for a pencil when Mark ignored the officer, jumped into his car, and accelerated down the snow-packed driveway. The security officer shook his head and put his ticket book and pencil away.

Mark stopped his car at the crossroads at the end of the hospital drive. As he tried to decide which way to turn, a snowplow entered the hospital drive. Mark opted for the direction from which the plow had come. He made the turn and drove into the night. As the car disappeared, there was no sound—not even the wind. Only the relentless snowfall.

Chapter 19

D avid stopped to take a breath and looked back the way he had just come. On the residential street leading up into the hills, all was quiet. The streets were empty, and nothing moved except the falling snow, which masked all sound. David listened to the profound silence for several minutes, and then, determined, he resumed his trek up the street. He was cold and clearly exhausted, but he plodded on. Numerous homes had Christmas lights burning, but most windows were already dark.

David felt dwarfed by his surroundings. Snow dusted his hair and eyebrows, and his breath came in visible spurts, like a miniature steam engine. To compensate for his fatigue and the cold, he retreated into his memories and continued to trudge toward the mountain.

First, David relived a Christmas past. He remembered his mom and dad under the mistletoe. Their embrace was warm and tender and lingering. David smiled longingly at the memory. He remembered his dad saying, "Merry Christmas, sweetheart. Thank you. I've wanted this—a family all my own—ever since I was a kid." In his memory, both parents looked toward David, smiled, and motioned for him to join them. "Come on, son. You're the one who makes us a family."

David recalled running into their arms and his parents playfully smothering him with kisses. He giggled as though he could still feel being tickled. Soon, the hugging turned into a wrestling match between him and Dad. He backed up a few paces and ran full tilt at his father. David's dad pretended to be knocked over backward. The boy pounced and sat on his dad's chest.

David strained to pin his father's shoulders to the ground, even though his dad offered only token resistance. The spectral David triumphed excitedly, "I gotcha! I gotcha!"

His dad feigned pain. "Ah! He's got me! Help! Help!"

David's mom gave a reasonable imitation of Jimmy Cagney. "All right, you guys! Let's get down to serious business!"

David shouted excitedly, "Presents!"

His mother looked at the ceiling in mock exasperation. "That too, but first—the birthday cakes."

The memory shifted in David's mind and candles from two small cakes stood in the center of his attention. The star filters of memory turned the candles into spectacular light displays. David was hazily aware of his parents in the background.

His mother asked, "Whose cake has the big candle?"

David responded, "Jesus', 'cause this is the day everyone picked to 'member his birthday."

His dad added, "And the other cake is just for you. Say, that's all right . . . two birthdays for the price of one. Pretty good deal, I'd say. Happy birthday, son, and Merry Christmas!"

In his memory of the event, David saw himself blow out the remaining candles. At that moment, the happy memory ended.

David was all alone in the snow. As he looked up at the streetlight, the curtain of snow created a halo that extended outward into the night.

When David came to the corner, he discovered he had reached the end of the houses on the street. The road continued for half a block up the hill, and then it ended abruptly. He looked wistfully at the last streetlight and turned his gaze out into the darkness. He was afraid. In the distance of the direction he was heading, David could see a stand of trees, bare and forbidding. Beyond that, barely visible in the reflected light of the town, the hill suddenly became a mountain.

Looking back the way he had just come, the dim lights of town seemed an impossible distance away. The falling snow gave the Christmas lights on the houses an unworldly glow. David was torn between his quest and his fear. Then, he remembered what the big bass had said at the church; "When the prophets wanted to talk to the Lord face to face, they got themselves up to a high mountain."

David paused for a moment. He took one last look at the streetlights and then turned and trudged into the night. The snow began to fall more heavily.

As David disappeared into the darkness, flakes began to fill his small footprints.

Chapter 20

Mark drove through the night, straining forward, trying to see out the windshield. He swiveled his head as he searched for any sign of his son. The depth of the snow made progress maddeningly slow. Suddenly, the car slipped as it fought for traction. Maintaining control became increasingly difficult, and fear-driven sweat broke out on Mark's forehead. Through clenched teeth, Mark pleaded with the car. "Come on . . . come on! You can't quit now!"

Bob Slovak continued to patrol off-duty in his car. He was now obsessed with finding the boy. Slovak played his spotlight into doorways and alleys as he passed. He let out a discouraged sigh and reached for the hand mike. "Dispatch, this is One-Charlie-Extra."

Immediately the dispatcher responded. "Go ahead,

One-Charlie-Extra. "

Slovak thought for a second and then keyed his mike.

"Any word on the missing boy? Over."

There was a hint of sadness in the dispatcher's response. "Negative."

The radio hissed for a moment, the carrier wave still open, and then, "One-Charlie-Extra, the watch commander advises no additional overtime has been authorized for your unit, over."

Slovak took a deep breath and responded. "Understood. Dispatch, show One-Charlie-Extra out of service but on the air. Request any updates on missing juvenile. One-Charlie-Extra clear."

The dispatcher was, once again, all business. "Copy, One-Charlie-Extra—dispatch clear."

The baker and his wife relaxed as best they could in their living room. They were surrounded by the trappings of an old-fashioned Christmas. Their furnishings, collected throughout their marriage, were from the Old World and their old lives. They had encircled themselves with artwork and carvings from the old country. Gretchen's collection of nutcrackers took up all the shelves along one wall. They appeared to stand at attention in artificial snow. Garlands of fresh pine were draped along each shelf, accented here and there with huge pinecones. A modest Christmas tree stood in the window, decorated with antique ornaments. Their traditional Christmas Eve celebration had been put on hold. Instead of joy and the companionship of neighbors and friends, there was an air of impending disaster.

Rolf was seated in his favorite overstuffed chair. He polished and repolished a large silver punch bowl. The matching silver cups were on the nearby table, but they remained unfilled and neglected; his mind was not on the work he was doing. His wife paced back and forth, alternately wringing her hands or wiping them with her apron. "Oh, Papa, that poor little boy . . . lost out there in the storm. What can we do?"

Without looking up he responded soberly, "We can only pray, Mama. That at least we can do, *ja?*"

Chapter 21

Father Powell sat uneasily on the couch in his mother's home. It should have been a time of rejoicing, but Father Powell felt no joy. Family and friends were present. The traditional Christmas buffet overwhelmed the dining room table, and most of the party members held nearly empty plates, which had previously overflowed with seasonal delights. Father Powell's full plate remained on his lap. He hadn't touched a thing. He just sat there staring at the fire, his right thumb twisting and stroking his right eyebrow. His younger brother, Paul, sat in front of the fire, his right leg and its thigh-high cast propped up on his mother's favorite footstool. Paul was the focus of attention, a position he clearly relished. He was in the middle of telling a story.

". . . There was absolutely no way I could get out of it. So I said, 'You're on! The first one down wins the fifty.' And zoom!"—Paul illustrated the start by skipping one hand off the other—"We were off! We were elbow to elbow into the last switchback when I cut the corner too fine, went over the edge, and rolled to the bottom. Charlie pulls up beside me, takes one look at this leg, and says, 'I'll get the ski patrol. You wait right here.' Right . . . as though I was going to run off somewhere." He beamed in response to the laughter from the group.

Mrs. Powell had been watching her son the priest throughout the story. She was troubled by his distant attitude and hardly heard a word as Paul delivered the punch line.

"I said, 'Not until I get the fifty you owe me! The bet was first one down—didn't say a thing about how we got here.'"

The family laughed and resumed their individual conversations. The family matriarch moved beside her oldest son. "Jonathan, what's troubling you?"

Father Powell looked in the general direction of his mother and refocused his attention. "What's that? Oh. I'm sorry, Mother. Something is nagging at me—something I missed."

"I could tell. Ever since you were little, you've always fiddled with your eyebrow when something bothers you."

"Hmm," he replied. Father Powell got to his feet and placed his uneaten food on the table. He kissed his mother on the forehead and poured a cup of eggnog. As he passed, his younger brother reached up and grabbed his coattail.

"Hey, big brother, you're looking a mite peaked. You ought to get out on the slopes. It'd do you a world of good."

Father Powell looked at Paul from under furrowed eyebrows. "We can all see it's done great things for you, Paul."

There were some good-natured chuckles from the family. Paul's face turned bright red as he struggled to his feet in a show of bravado. Heatedly, he challenged, "I'll bet I can still beat you down the hill, cast and all!"

Father Powell looked at the cast in mock solemnity. "I keep telling you, little brother, gambling's a sin. It's going to cause you a lot of pain one of these days . . . or has it already?"

Paul sputtered. Their mother stepped in and issued a good-natured rebuke. "Stop it, you two! You still act like little kids every time you get together . . . trying to get one up on each other. You, Paul, a *mature*—" she placed heavy emphasis on the word—"businessman trying to act like you're still a young college student. You should have more self-respect—more dignity."

"Yes, Mother."

"And you, Jonathan, a man of the cloth, still trying to needle your younger brother like some school-yard tease. You should listen to some of your own sermons on patience and brotherly love."

"Yes, Mother." Then, with a wink at his brother, he

added, "Just like old times, eh, little brother?"

Paul laughed in spite of himself. "Just like old times, big brother."

Father Powell moved over to the rest of the family and gave his younger sister, Mary, an affectionate kiss on the cheek. "Merry Christmas, little sister. It's nice having the family all together."

Mary was having a hard time suppressing a laugh. "Merry Christmas, Jonathan. I thought for a minute you and Paul were going to get down on the rug and wrestle like you used to."

"Yes, well, it was tempting, but Mother put the shut to that in a hurry."

Mary laughed openly now. "She's still a pretty formidable foe. I'll bet she still has that old willow switch in the hall closet."

Father Powell smiled and rubbed an imaginary sore spot on his rump. "If she doesn't, she'd cut one soon enough."

Fred Carver, a long-time neighbor, wandered over. He listened for a moment and asked a totally irrelevant question. "Well, Father Powell, is Notre Dame going to win the national title?"

Father Powell responded with good-natured humor. "Well, Fred, Paul could probably quote the odds, but . . . Lord willing and the creek don't rise and the S.C. running back doesn't have a Heisman Trophy afternoon, chances are pretty fair."

The children tumbled into the room excitedly. They were dressed for the annual Christmas story. Their mothers made last minute adjustments to their costumes, and one or two received whispered reminders about their cue-lines. Three of the children carried broom handles on which stuffed camel heads had been affixed. The make-believe camels suddenly became weapons, and a minor skirmish broke out. Their respective mothers quickly grabbed the combatants, and the war ended in unconditional surrender.

A couple of the fathers made their way to the buffet table to fortify themselves with coffee and a piece of pie. Father Powell fished in his coat pocket for his reading glasses.

The children had been waiting with great anticipation for this annual event. Excitedly, they talked over each other as they scrambled for their places. "Come on, Father Powell! It's time for the Christmas story! Time for Mary and Joseph!"

The children grabbed Father Powell by the hand and dragged him into the living room. He smiled at them and allowed himself to be seated in a large armchair next to the family Bible. The rest of the family gathered, the men bringing chairs from the dining room.

Father Powell adjusted his reading glasses, took the Bible in hand, and turned to the verse he had chosen.

He was always deeply moved by Saint Luke's account, so he began with emotion, "And it came to pass in those days, that there went out a decree from Caesar Augustus, that all in the world should be taxed. And all went to be taxed every one into his own city. And Joseph also went up . . ."

Father Powell peered over his reading glasses at the boy dressed as Joseph. The boy's mother prodded him, and he shyly took his place in the tableau. The other children giggled until a stern look from Father Powell silenced them. He continued:

"And Joseph also went up from Galilee, out of the city of Nazareth, into Judea, unto the city of David, which is called Bethlehem; to be taxed with Mary his espoused wife, being great with child."

The little girl dressed as Mary slipped into her place. Shepherds and wise men, complete with false beards, stood by, waiting eagerly for their cue. Father Powell smiled at the surrogate Mary and settled back into his chair.

"And so it was, that, while they were there, the days were accomplished that she should be delivered. And she brought forth her firstborn son, and wrapped him in swaddling clothes, and laid him in a manger; because there was no room for them in the inn." He paused mid-quote and cleared his throat. "No room for them . . ."

Father Powell removed his reading glasses and sat silent for a moment. He twisted and stroked his right eyebrow as he thought. The children looked at each other in bewilderment. The adults looked at each other in alarm.

Concerned, his mother whispered, "Jonathan . . . ?"

Tears streamed down Father Powell's face. He set the

Bible back in its place, wiped his eyes, and got to his feet.

In muffled tones he explained, "I'm sorry, Mother. I . . . I think I made a terrible mistake earlier tonight, and I've got to see if I can make it right."

Father Powell grabbed his coat and muffler from the closet, opened the door, and put them on amid questions from his family. "You're not leaving!" "What about the Christmas story?" "Why so soon? Mass doesn't start for hours!" After his hasty exit, the family was left behind staring at each other.

Father Powell's mother was deeply disturbed. "I've never seen him like this." She moved to the window and watched as her firstborn drove away from the curb.

Chapter 22

David was totally alone as he struggled to walk through the curtain of snow. The powder was now deep enough that he sank almost to his knees with every step. It was an exhausting process just to keep going. His misery was compounded by the memory of those people he had stopped to ask for help as he had walked the streets on his quest. They taunted him anew as he pictured them in his mind. Their images were somewhat distorted, but he remembered the emotions he felt when he had confronted each of them on the street.

The specter of a well-dressed man stopped, leaned over, and listened for a moment. David could hear the echo of his own voice asking, "Please, sir, can you tell me where I can find Jesus?"

The well-dressed man waved his hand at the sky and walked on. His tone made it clear that he was annoyed by the question. "Jesus? Probably on a cloud somewhere."

A middle-aged woman holding a shopping bag immediately replaced the man's fading image. She frowned at David, and then turned and pointed in the direction from which she has just come. "What a question!" she exclaimed, "I suppose he's in a church somewhere."

Throngs of people passed by, unmindful of the boy. Their packages banged into him as the tears began to flow.

Two women were walking together. The first woman reached out a hand and patted David on the head as though he were a puppy. They walked on without stopping or answering his question. One of the women who patted David turned to her companion. "Isn't he sweet?" she gushed.

Next, David remembered a Salvation Army worker ringing his bell by a kettle. The uniformed man looked down at David, smiled warmly, and, without breaking the rhythm of the bell, placed his left hand over his heart and said sincerely, "He needs to be in our hearts, little boy."

The Salvation Army worker faded and was replaced in David's memory by the specter of a pompous minister who smiled down at him condescendingly. He responded to David's question by dramatically spreading his hands in a sweeping motion toward the sky, saying, "He's everywhere!"

Next, three teenagers strutted toward David. The leader leaned back as though listening to David's question. Then, he shoved his nose right into David's face, wagged his head from side to side, and responded rudely, "Jesus! He's nowhere! Ha, ha, har!" With that, the three teenagers swaggered on, laughing and punching each other on the shoulder.

As the memories faded, David stopped, waved his arms, and shook his head as though he were contending with someone. Then, as though answering those phantoms, he cried out, "No! He's real! My parents told me . . . he's our friend."

Then he was alone . . . a little boy lost in the snow. He tried to take a few more steps. Each one required a supreme effort. Finally, he dropped to his knees in the snow. Below him were the lights of the town. Those distant lights made him feel all the more alone. David's head drooped. He snapped his head up, fighting off sleep.

Then, slowly, carefully, he folded his arms. Sleepily, but earnestly, he spoke as his parents had taught him. "Dear Heavenly Father, I know you're busy and all . . . but I've tried so hard to find Jesus, and soon it will be Chris'mas. And by then it'll be too late."

David's head drooped again. With increasing difficulty he fought against sleep. As if to convince himself to continue his mission he mumbled, "So many things to tell him . . . need my mommy . . . my dad needs . . . don't need presents . . . just my mommy . . . but I'm . . . so tired and it's so cold. . . ."

From the perspective of the snow-capped mountain, all that could be seen against the pristine powder was David, alone in the snow. The only tracks to be seen were his. And they were filling fast.

Father Powell drove through the snow, looking for something, but he had no idea what. He stopped, looked around, rolled down the window, and listened.

Chapter 23

Kelly Green paced like a caged animal behind the broad-cast console. He looked at his collection of Pepsi bottles for a moment and framed them with his hands like an artist examining his work. Then he walked over to where he had stacked a collection of wadded-up paper balls. He scooped them up and then, spinning around, made a series of different shots into a wastepaper basket. He didn't miss a single shot. He then pantomimed getting high-fives from imaginary teammates.

"Eat your heart out, NBL! Oh, Kelly me boy-o, you're a champ! Why didn't you try out?"

From behind him came a reply, "Because you're only six foot two and a half on your best days . . . and because you've got white man's disease." Kelly spun and found Dwight, the station's six-foot-four chief engineer leaning in the doorway to the studio.

Dwight had recently returned from Europe, where he functioned as chief engineer for Armed Forces Radio. He held the distinction of being the first Negro non-com assigned to the Signal Corps prior to the Normandy invasion. Dwight held a six-pack of Pepsi and a pizza. Kelly nodded in agreement as Dwight and Kelly finished the thought simultaneously. "You're slow, I'm slow!"

Dwight entered the studio and deposited the goodies on the table. He looked closely at a current Pepsi ad Kelly had pinned up in the studio, shook his head, held up a Pepsi bottle, and asked, "Kelly, why don't you just insert an IV and inject this stuff? You know, like the plasma the medics gave wounded troops during the war. You'd save time and money."

Kelly held up his hand imperiously to silence Dwight. He then opened a bottle of Pepsi, using a brass bottle opener affixed under the master console. First, he sniffed the brown liquid and then tasted it, as one might a fine wine. Expansively, he spoke as if to a serf. "Silence, peasant! Yes . . .a good year . . . but not, I'm afraid, a great year."

"Nut!" Dwight snorted in disgust.

Kelly looked hurt. "I've invited you to this elaborate Yuletide feast, and how do you repay me? With insults! I'll have you know, *this* is the national beverage." Without missing a beat, he slapped a small disk on the nearest turntable and flipped the switch to audition.

From the overhead speakers came the famous jazz version of the Pepsi Jingle . . . .

"Pepsi Cola hits the spot; twelve full ounces, that's a lot. Twice as much for a nickel too, Pepsi Cola is the drink for you! Nickel, nickel, nickel, nickel, nickel, nickel, nickel, nickel . . . Trickle, trickle, trickle, trickle, Trickle, trickle, trickle, trickle . . . "

Under his breath, Dwight reiterated, "Nut!"

Kelly responded in a matter of fact manner. "Have some pizza."

The two men dug in.

Kelly periodically checked the clock. He looked at the wastebasket wistfully. " 'Tis a shame, it is. I may be slow but I'm a great shot."

Dwight wiped his mouth with a paper towel. "Let me guess. You want to try out with the first place Fort Wayne Zollner Pistons. They 'only' scored 78 points against the Dayton Acmes. That's the highest point total since the World Professional Basketball Tournament was founded in '39. I'm sure you can convince them they need you."

Kelly shrugged. "Yeah, but the MVP, Buddy Janette, only scored 18 points."

Dwight broke out laughing. "Don't forget, MVP Sonny Boswell of the Harlem Globetrotters only scored 12 points in 1940. They haven't been contenders since. Maybe you should try out with the Trotters."

Kelly held out his pale hands and thought for a minute. Then, sadly, he conceded, "Maybe I should stick with radio."

"Not a bad thought," Dwight said with a chuckle. "Besides," he added, "look at all the side benefits. Not to mention," he said sarcastically, "the great hours."

Kelly shrugged. "Hey, Dwight, how'd you get into broadcasting anyway? Weren't you some kind of jock in high school?"

Dwight shook his head with finality. "Not a chance! My daddy decided that for me before I was born."

Kelly seemed floored. "You're kidding."

"Nope. It seems when my daddy was a boy in Hoboken, the Dempsey–Carpentier championship fight was being broadcast over the wireless for the first time in history. Tickets to the Jersey City fight were going for $5.50 apiece—a fortune in those days. My daddy first heard they were going to broadcast the fight when the newspaper ran a story about GE bringing the transmitter down the Hudson River on a barge to the Lackawanna Terminal at Hoboken. He found out that amateur radio operators up to 350 miles away were allowed to receive the broadcast for audiences gathered in theater halls in sixty-some cities. Dad told me they took up collections to benefit the Navy and Marine Corps. I think some of the money went to help the people in war-devastated France. Anyway, it was a big deal."

"That's interesting," Kelly interjected, "but what's that got to do with you?"

Dwight chuckled. "Everything! My daddy worked all day setting up chairs at one of the halls to earn his ticket to the broadcast. While everybody was listening to the fight, Daddy hovered over the radio receiver, asking questions until the operator finally told him to get lost. From that time on, he was hooked.

"When I was born, Daddy gave me a crystal set instead of a teddy bear. From the time I can first remember, he and I were taking apart old radios and putting them back together again. In high school, I joined the radio club and learned how radio worked. When the war came, I was drafted into the Army and ended up in the Signal Corps. I got transferred to London and assigned to the Armed Forces Network. I've never told anyone this, Kelly, but I was there on the Fourth of July when Corporal Syl Binkin became the first military broadcaster ever heard over the air." Embarrassed at the disclosure of all this personal information, Dwight cut his answer short. "The rest, as they say, is history."

Kelly was genuinely impressed. "Wow," he offered profoundly.

Dwight laughed out loud and asked, "Okay, Mr. Announcer Sir, how did you break into this crazy business?"

"I always listened to Arthur Godfrey. I even heard his account of FDR's funeral when he broke down on the air. I thought his down-home, straight-talking style was the future of radio. Most of the station managers I worked for thought I was nuts. When AM-570 picked up Godfrey in this market, I went to this station's management and convinced them to let me try a prime time, five-day-a-week, live local talk show to counter Godfrey." Then, with a twinkle his eye, Kelly added, "The rest, as they say, is history."

Dwight gave Kelly a curious look. "Speaking of which, we engineers work crazy hours 'cause that's the only time we can do maintenance on the transmitter. But you! How did a prime time talk jock end up riding herd on a stack of Christmas carols?"

Kelly wiped pizza sauce off his mouth and chin. "I made the mistake of volunteering. I'm single, the other guys are married. My folks are gone. . . . Anyway, I traded for New Year's Eve off. Plus, I thought we'd do a late night talk bit with the lonelies and the insomniacs. But the boss said no. He made it crystal clear . . . on Christmas Eve, we don't talk—we play carols. So . . . ."

Dwight yawned. "How exciting."

Kelly shook his head. "Boring! Do me a favor. Old 'Rip 'n' Read Rick' didn't leave me any news clips when he split. See if there's anything on the wire I can use to liven things up. A nice juicy murder would be just the thing."

Dwight moved to the news printer. "You're sick! Why do I put up with you?"

Kelly held up a sagging slice. "I bribe you with pizza." The last carol in the series ended. Kelly punched up the next series.

Chapter 24

ob Slovak stopped his car by the side of the road. He leaned his left elbow on his right arm and rested his forehead on his left fist. With closed eyes, he prayed. "I'm not very good at this, sir, and I'm not asking for myself, but please—please help that little boy."

Bob Slovak opened his eyes, looked around as though he was afraid he'd been seen praying, and then drove on.

Rolf Liesel and his wife were huddled together in their living room. Outside, a gust of wind rattled some branches against the windowpane and the side of the house, but they were oblivious to the sound. They knelt, holding hands, engaged in fervent prayer for the safety of a little boy they had seen only once.

At the radio station, Dwight stuck his head in the studio and extended a sheaf of wire service copy. "Sorry, no murderers. A couple of juicy political things, though . . . and there's a local kid lost out in the storm. That could be a rough one. Take a look at the weather report. Brutal!"

Kelly grabbed the material, glanced through it, and shook his head. "Oh man, that little guy won't last long when the temperature drops . . . poor kid. This is the kind of thing that makes you wish you could do something besides talking about it."

Dwight looked at the announcer as though seeing him for the first time.

Father Powell looked carefully out his car window as he drove through the nearly deserted streets. The grim and determined look on his face was far removed from the jovial parish priest. He switched on the radio, listened for a second, and then switched it off just as a carol was ending. He stopped the car, turned off the motor, rolled down the window, and listened. His eyes searched the night, uncertain what it was he sought. Then, in frustration, he gave voice to what had been a silent prayer. "What is it, Lord? I feel you prodding me. I'm trying to listen, but I don't know what you want me to do!"

He rolled up the window, started the car, and began moving again. Idly, he switched the radio back on. The announcer was in the middle of a newscast. " . . . By a three-vote margin, thus upholding the governor's veto. On the local front, police are still searching for the six-year-old boy last seen in the downtown area earlier this afternoon. He is described as three feet ten inches tall, blond with blue eyes, and last seen wearing a light blue jacket. Anyone with information is urged to call local authorities."

Father Powell gunned his car into a gas station and slid to a stop next to a telephone booth.

Caroline had been pacing up and down in front of the telephone in Mark and David's house for what seemed like hours. She stopped, reached for the phone, checked herself, and resumed pacing. Whiskers paced for a few steps too and then sat on her haunches and waited to see what this crazy human would do next. One of David's toys lay abandoned nearby.

After a short coffee break, Bob Slovak resumed off-duty patrol. He rearranged himself in the seat as though expecting a long night. The police radio was silent, so he turned on the AM radio.

" . . . Best buys in snow tires is at Sears Auto Center."

The report continued. "One of the legends of the Second World War was laid to rest today. General George Patton, who ironically made it through countless battles only to succumb to injuries suffered in a traffic accident, was buried with full military honors this Christmas Eve."

Slovak turned off the radio and looked out into the night. *Old Blood and Guts,* he thought. *You were one of a kind, sir . . . but I suspect you'll have to watch your language from now on.*

The police radio came to life. "Dispatch to One-Charlie-Extra . . . ."

Slovak grabbed the microphone and responded immediately, "One-Charlie-Extra. Go!"

The dispatcher seemed distracted and busy. Slovak heard other calls in the background. "One-Charlie-Extra. See a party at the Chevron station, corner of 6th and Main, regarding the missing child."

Slovak responded automatically. "Copy! I'm en route. One-Charlie-Extra out!"

Slovak checked his mirror, and seeing no traffic, he spun his car in the middle of the street and reversed his direction.

Chapter 25

David knelt motionless and half-buried in the snow, his head bowed in the attitude of prayer. Suddenly, the area directly around David grew brighter and brighter until it was as bright as day. Within the confines of that light, no snow fell.

Through the depths of sleep, David heard a voice calling him. The voice was deep and rich, yet very gentle. "Son . . . wake up."

David stirred but did not wake. He closed his eyes even tighter in reaction to the light that washed over him.

Again, the voice called to him, "David, wake up."

Slowly, David opened his eyes. He squinted into the bright light and put up a hand to shield his eyes so he could see.

David felt a pair of powerful arms lifting him up. They belonged to a man whose clothing was so brilliantly white, it was almost impossible to look at. The lines were simple but elegant. There was no color to distract the eye.

David's head came to rest on the man's shoulder. The boy wrapped his arms around his benefactor and rested there for a moment. Then he pulled back and looked intently at the man. David felt no fear, only curiosity.

The man's hair and beard were naturally curly, like lamb's wool, and both were as white as snow. David was intrigued because, in spite of the white hair and beard, this man didn't seem any older than David's dad. He felt secure in the arms of this stranger because there was something familiar about him.

David tilted his head slightly, reached out a hand, and very gently ran his fingers over the side of the man's beard. He smiled as he discovered it was just as soft as he thought it would be. Suddenly, David remembered his mission. "Is it Christmas yet?"

There was a smile in the stranger's voice. "No, there's still time."

David struggled to get down. "I gotta hurry! It's important! I gotta find someone before Christmas."

The response was firm but gentle. "David, I am the One you seek."

David looked closely at the Lord's face. "Are you . . . ?"

He nodded.

David hugged him tighter. And then, sobbing, he poured his heart out. "I've looked *everywhere* for you. No one would tell me how to find you. I don't need birthday presents or

Christmas presents. I just need my mommy. . . ."

As David wept, the mountain remained unmoved. Immediately outside the light that surrounded them, the heavy snowfall continued. The only sound heard on the mountain was the moaning of the wind.

At last, the Lord set David down. He then lowered himself to the boy's height and explained the purpose of mortality to the boy.

David listened intently as he was given the answers he so desperately sought.

". . . and if she'd stayed with you, the pain would have become so terrible she wouldn't even have known you."

David shook his head, trying very hard to understand.

"She didn't want you to see that."

With the logic of the innocent, David asked the question that countless millions have pondered over the centuries. "But why did she have to have pain? Couldn't you make it go away?"

The Lord gently nodded his head. "There is a great pain, which I have accepted, to take away the suffering of others. Do you remember your father telling you about that?"

David nodded eagerly.

"But physical pain is part of life. It teaches, it protects, and sometimes, as in your mother's case, it comes with illness. Sometimes the test of life includes a great deal of pain. But your mother has passed that test. And now she's well and happy. You should be very proud of her."

"Does my mommy miss me?" David asked. "Can I see her?"

The Lord reached out to reassure the little boy. David noticed marks in his wrist and hand. "You remember my telling you that, during life, everyone has to make their own choices?"

David nodded solemnly.

"You have made a great sacrifice to plead your case. You have been heard and your prayers have been carefully weighed. If you so choose, you can be with your mother now . . . "

The little boy broke into a broad grin.

"But, David, your mother is very wise, and she hopes you'll stay to help and comfort your father. She wants you to grow up to be like him—a loving man, with a family of your own. That is her earnest prayer. In time, you'll all be together again. But there are still many important things for you to do."

David watched closely as the Lord stood. David's head moved to follow. "The choice is yours, David. Consider carefully what your parents want for you and why. Now, my son, it's time for you to choose."

David pondered his choice for a moment. "Can I see my mommy now?"

The mountain remained indifferent. The pair was just a bright square of light against its stark landscape.

Chapter 26

A single lit window in Grace Baptist Church caught Mark's attention as he slowly traversed the street for the tenth time. As he slowly moved down the street, the light went out, and Mark saw two men coming down the stairs. He passed them, but then, on an impulse, he slammed on the brakes. His car slid sideways as he opened the door and jumped out, leaving the vehicle running and the door flung open in the middle of the street.

Biggs the choir director and Don the bass stood at the foot of the stairs. They looked at each other, both anticipating some kind of confrontation.

Mark held up his hands to show he meant no harm. Urgently, he pleaded, "Please . . . I'm just looking for my little boy. He's lost."

Biggs glanced at Don and then at this stranger who had just accosted them. "What does he look like, your little boy?"

Mark hurried over. He held out his hand to indicate height. "About that high, blond . . . he's wearing a light blue jacket."

The choir director and Don looked at each other again, frowning.

Mark looked from one to the other. Impatiently, he demanded, "What? Have you seen him. What is it?"

Biggs responded with measured calm. "If it was your boy, he didn't exactly seem lost. It was more like he was searching for something . . . or someone."

Mark was nearly frantic. "He recently lost his mother. His aunt told him his mother had gone to live with Jesus. He doesn't understand. In the name of God, man, if you know anything, please tell me!"

Don was stricken. He responded with a prayer, not an oath. "Oh, dear, sweet Jesus! I told that child that when the prophets wanted to talk to the Lord, they went to the mountains!"

"I don't understand," Mark said.

The bass pointed in the direction of the mountains. In his resonant tones, he answered, "I think your boy has gone up into the hills."

Mark bolted for his car. He jammed it in gear before even closing the door.

"Wait!" the choir director called after him. "We'll help!"

Both men watched Mark's car make a sliding turn at the next corner before rushing for their own cars. Biggs stopped abruptly and slammed one gloved fist into his other hand. He tried to think clearly. "Wait! This may take some time. We've got to call our families. . . . If we don't, you can bet they'll have search parties out looking for us. The last thing we want to do is add to the problem."

Don nodded, and both men rushed back up to the church, taking the stairs two at a time. Biggs fumbled with his keys and finally got the door open. Both men hurried to the small office in back of the choir stand. Biggs grabbed the phone and dialed home.

His son answered formally, exactly as he'd been trained to do. "Franklin residence, this is Matthew. May I help you?"

Biggs was pleased but impatient. "Good boy, Matthew, you did that very well . . . let me speak to Mommy . . . yes, I know it's almost Christmas, but Daddy has to speak to Mommy." He rubbed his forehead in frustration. "Son! Get your mother! Now!"

Again, he rubbed his head as he waited. When his wife finally came on the line, she immediately demanded an explanation as to why he wasn't home yet.

"Judith . . . no, I'm still here. Judith . . . something's happened. That little boy who came with Joshua . . . yes, that's the one. Well, he's lost out in the hills. We're going to help search. It may take several hours . . . yes, I know, but what if it were Matthew? . . . I will. Can you call Mary Beth? I think she'd want to know. Yes . . . as soon as I can." He pressed the cradle to disconnect and handed the phone to Don.

Chapter 27

Mary Beth, Joshua's mother, hummed a lullaby as she tucked her precocious son into bed. She turned off the overhead lights and snapped on a small cherubic lamp that acted as a night-light. In its soft warm glow, she reached out and ran her hand through her son's hair. *He's so much like his daddy*, she thought as she watched him yawn and snuggle his head in the pillow. The lullaby seemed to be working. Then, all of a sudden, Joshua's eyes popped wide open, and he looked panicked. "I forgot to put out cookies and milk!"

His mother smiled reassuringly. "Hush now. I'll see to it. You go to sleep. The sooner you do, the sooner you'll see your presents."

Joshua seemed puzzled. "Why's that? If it's the same time, how come going to bed early makes it shorter?" Mary Beth was both amused and amazed at her curious offspring. "Well, Joshua, it just *seems* shorter because—" The phone rang. "You just go to sleep. We'll talk about it in the morning." Mary Beth gave Joshua a quick kiss on the forehead and then rose to answer the phone.

She picked up the receiver, glanced at the clock, and answered cautiously, "Hello? . . . Oh, good evening, Judith . . . yes . . . oh, no . . . no! . . . Are they sure?" Mary Beth was deeply concerned. "That poor little boy. . . . I'm glad you did. . . . of course we will." She hung up the phone and stood there for moment, troubled by the call. She turned to find Joshua standing nearby, rubbing his eyes sleepily. He rested his head against a large teddy bear he was holding, yawned, and asked, "Who's that?"

Mary Beth sat on the floor next to her son and gathered him into her arms. She found it difficult to keep the concern she felt out of her voice. "Oh, Joshua . . . your little friend . . . he's lost somewhere out there in the storm."

Joshua looked at his mother. He felt scared as he slowly grasped what was happening. "I wish Daddy were here." Joshua whispered. "He'd know what to do."

Mary Beth looked at the hall table where a picture of her husband stood. He was a tall, handsome officer dressed in flight gear. In the picture, he stood in front of a P-51 Mustang and looked skyward over his right shoulder. His goggles were pulled back on the forehead of his canvas flight helmet and his Mae West was worn over his khaki flying blouse. The captain's bars on his collar marked him as an elite member of a select group.

"Yes Josh . . . yes, he would."

Chapter 28

Father Powell sat in the passenger seat of the patrol car beside Bob Slovak. Both men strained to see through the heavy snow. Father Powell was deeply engrossed in brooding thought. Slovak glanced at him every few minutes, wondering what the priest was thinking.

Father Powell, more to himself than to Slovak, answered the unspoken question. "How could I have let myself become so smug, so . . . so *comfortable* in my calling? Can you imagine? I was patting myself on the back for just doing my job when this little guy comes to me and asks where he can find Jesus. 'More important business,' I said. I oughtta turn in this collar for a tin cup! A blind man would have known better than to send him out there in the snow."

Slovak listened with a growing sense of guilt. "I did the same thing."

The priest turned to the big cop and refocused his attention. "How's that?"

"I sent him out in the snow too." He shook his head in frustration. "He was that close!" he said, his arm outstretched to show the distance. "But I sent him away . . . to you."

Father Powell slumped deeper in his seat and hunched his shoulders. "What a pair we make!" Angrily, he looked at his watch. "What am I going to do? Midnight mass is my responsibility, but so is this boy."

Father Powell was clearly torn. Slovak grimly checked his mirrors, looked over his shoulder, and executed a tight u-turn at the intersection.

"I'll drop you at the church," Slovak said midway through the turn. "Right now, we need all the prayers we can get."

Mark banged on his steering wheel in frustration. No matter what he did, his car wouldn't go any faster. He leaned forward, scowling out at the night sky through the snow-clad windshield. The snowfall was now so heavy that it had become almost impossible to see to the end of his headlights. Prayerfully he pleaded, "Dear Lord, please don't let me be too late."

Biggs and Don had decided to drive separate cars to widen the search. At an intersection, they stopped in tandem.

Biggs jumped out and ran over to the other car. Don rolled down his window.

Pointing at fresh tire tracks in the snow, Biggs called out, "Looks like the boy's daddy went up this street. I'll take the next street on the left. You take the right.

Don nodded. "Got it!"

Biggs started back to his car on the run. Don called out, to him, "Wait!"

Biggs stopped in his tracks. Don leaned partway out his window. "These three streets are the only ones that go up into the hills," Don said. "He must've taken one of 'em. If you don't find him, cut toward the middle. I'll do the same."

Biggs waved his agreement and sprinted for his car. Both men drove on, their tires kicking up a flurry of snow. Somewhat recklessly, they each turned onto their assigned streets.

Slovak approached the intersection as two cars slid through their respective turns. One just barely missed Slovak's patrol car on the left, and the other weaved by in the other direction, nearly out of control.

Slovak skillfully avoided a collision, but the close call made him furious. "What the h— Er, sorry, Father."

Under his breath, Father Powell muttered, "I absolve you."

Slovak hit the switch for his light bar and punched the siren button. It gave a single "whoop."

The tires of the car ahead began spinning and then slid backwards into the gutter, directly in front of the patrol car.

Through clenched teeth, Slovak bit off a curse. "Wonderful!" he exclaimed in disgust.

Don jumped out of his car and sprinted toward Slovak's window. Out of breath, he tried to explain. "Officer, I'm part of a search party . . . a little boy lost in this storm. We think he's gone up in the hills on one of these roads . . . the other two are covered. I'm supposed to search that one up ahead."

Slovak nodded and exited the patrol car. "C'mon, Father. Let's get this Good Samaritan out of the ditch, and we'll help cover his street."

While Don spun the wheels, Slovak and Father Powell shoved him back on the road. Once again, Bob's pants were splattered with slush, but this time, he didn't seem to care. Don rolled down his window, leaned out, and in the reflected flashing light from the patrol car, he waved his thanks. He moved cautiously up the road.

Slovak watched Father Powell anxiously glance at his watch and start tugging at his eyebrow. Slovak yelled at the retreating car, "Hold it!" He ran toward the car, waving at Father Powell to follow. "Come on, Father, hustle!"

The two reached the driver's side of Don's car, and Slovak

yanked open the door to confront a startled Don. Pointing at his badge, Slovak said abruptly, "Sorry! I need to commandeer this vehicle." He dragged the sputtering driver out from behind the wheel.

"Take it, Father. There's still time. Just drive carefully. Have someone stand by the phone, and we'll call the minute there's news."

Father Powell hesitated for a second, so Slovak shoved him toward the open door.

Don, bewildered, sputtered, "But I . . . ."

Impatiently, Slovak led the confused man toward his patrol car. Starting the engine, he explained, "He's got a mass to celebrate, and we've got a boy to find. You can ride with me . . . unless you don't trust him with your car."

Don grinned sheepishly. "Be my guest."

Father Powell leaned out the open window. "Find him," he entreated soberly.

Chapter 29

Mark approached the end of the street. His tires were losing traction, and his progress slowed to a walking pace. He slammed on the parking brake and killed the engine. The night was deathly still. The snow had stopped, and a brilliant moon broke through the clouds. Mark leaned across the seat to reach into the glove compartment. At first, he didn't find what he was looking for. In frustration, he started yanking things out of the glove compartment. At last, he found the flashlight he was looking for. He tested it, banging it on the dashboard when it didn't work. Finally, it flickered and came to life.

Mark exited the car, looked at the sky, and gave silent thanks that the snow had finally stopped. He swept the light on the far side of the street and saw nothing. He worked his way to the near side of the road, the flashlight beam sweeping the snow before him. As he swung the light back and forth, it passed by a series of slight depressions. He brought the light back close and froze on the nearest depression. It resembled what Slovak had shown him earlier at Father Powell's church. In the reflected light, Mark's face showed a mixture of excitement and fear. His accelerated breathing was visible in the cold. He leaned over and blew light powder out of the icy cast. There, in the snow, was the unmistakable footprint of his missing son. Mark sprang to his feet and started up the hill.

Mark felt as though he were running in slow motion. Clumps of snow, kicked up by his feet, glistened in the moonlight. Still, he ran at full speed, holding nothing in reserve. He was soon exhausted, but he wouldn't allow himself to stop. The adrenaline that drove him quickly burned the last of his energy reserves. His strength ebbed, and soon his legs refused to support him. He fell to his hands and knees in the snow, gasping for breath and pleading for strength, "No! Please . . . help me!"

Bob Slovak and Don the bass made slow progress through the high drifts. Slovak pointed off in the distance where the boy's father could be seen in the moonlight.

Slovak, between breaths, shouted, "He was running, but he's down!"

Don added excitedly, "I think he found something."

Slovak nodded, changed direction, and picked up the pace.

Mark forced himself to his feet, staggered, and, by sheer force of will, managed to place one foot in front of the other, relentlessly following his little boy's tracks. Totally exhausted, he looked at the hillside ahead and saw that the depressions he had been following ended abruptly at a small mound in the snow. His face was a mask of horror. Through clenched teeth he cried out.

A new surge of fear triggered Mark's remaining adrenaline. He plowed through the snow at a dead run, finally dropping to his knees beside the tiny mound. The brilliant moon cast a cold blue light on the tragic scene.

Frantically, Mark snatched his son from the snowy cocoon and clutched him to his breast. The little boy lay limp and motionless in his father's arms. He was the color of alabaster. Mark ripped off his earmuffs and jammed his ear against his son's chest. He held that position as if frozen in time. Eventually, he rocked back on his knees and clenched his teeth, throwing his head back as though he were a wolf baying at the moon. He vented one long and anguished cry into the night.

Slovak's group stumbled to a halt as the grief-stricken cry echoed across the hillside. Don dropped to his knees and began sobbing openly. He pounded his own leg as if punishing himself.

Slovak's face took on the granite mask he always wore as a police officer. He moved toward the distant figure in the snow.

Don, hoarse and breathless, called him to a halt. "No. Leave him in his grief. There's no hurry . . . not now." Slovak nodded and dropped in the snow to rest, panting to catch his breath.

Across the field, the choir director stood at a respectful distance. He covered his face with his hand as if not wanting to face the outcome.

Mark sobbed from the depths of his soul as he clutched his only son to his heart and rocked him back and forth. He cried out in agony. "My son, my son! Oh Lord, my God, it's more than I can bear. You don't know how I suffer!"

Mark's body was wracked with sobs. His soul was filled with the bitter cold of despair. The implacable mountain offered no pity. At that ashen moment, when it seemed to Mark as though he had been totally abandoned and bereft of all that he loved, a deep, rich voice responded to his cry. Mark both felt it in his heart and heard it in his mind.

I know and understand. Was not my Son as deeply loved as thine? Be still and know that I am.

At that moment, distant bells cried out, signalling the coming of Christmas morn, and a small hand reached up to wipe away his father's tears.

In a moment, Mark's sobs turned to joyous laughter. He grabbed his son's hand and held it to his cheek.

David looked as though he was waking from a long sleep. Drowsily, he smiled up at his dad. "I saw Mommy . . . she looked so happy. She still loves us very much. Is it Christmas yet?

Mark struggled to his feet, holding his son tightly to him as he answered joyfully, "Yes! Yes! Listen."

In the distance, more bells cried out the good tidings. It was a jubilant sound. Mark stood with his son in his arms and spun around in a joyous circle. "It's Christmas morning! Happy birthday, David!"

David smiled sleepily. "Happy birthday, Jesus."

Biggs raised his head slowly as he heard Mark's laughter. He tilted his head to one side, as if trying to understand what he was hearing. Then the reality of the situation dawned on him, and he leaped to his feet and began to run.

As Mark's laughter reached Slovak and Don, the two men looked at each other in disbelief. Don struggled to his feet and offered a reverent and awed prayer of thanks. "Thank thee, Lord!" Slovak and Don took off on a dead run toward the exultant parent.

As the rescue teams reached the father and son, they

grabbed the pair and joined in the celebration, dancing around in a widening circle of joy.

Bob Slovak stepped away from the group for a moment, took out his portable radio, a war surplus walkie-talkie, and keyed the mike. Excited and breathless, he called in, "Dispatch, One-Charlie-Extra!"

"One-Charlie-Extra. Go."

Trying to maintain some amount of professionalism in spite of his relief, he said, "The boy has been found. He's alive. Repeat. The boy has been found alive."

"Copy, One-Charlie-Extra. Are you requesting a rescue unit?"

Slovak's granite face broke into a broad smile. "Negative, dispatch. We will transport to nearest medical facility. Please notify the rest of the family, and call the cathedral. They're waiting to hear. Then call all interested parties. Tell them . . . tell them Merry Christmas!"

The group of rescuers moved down the hillside, crowded together as they lent a hand to Mark, who carried his son.

Don, with tears of thanksgiving on his face, sang quietly to himself, "Thank thee, O Lord, for the safe return of this little one."

Biggs wore a smile of deep satisfaction and formulated in his mind a report on this modern miracle, which he would share with the congregation later that day.

David was tired, but he smiled with great warmth and snuggled against his father.

Mark had a hard time maintaining his composure. He periodically placed his cheek against his son's for reassurance. For the first time, Mark fully registered the presence of the rest of the rescue party. Breathing hard with exertion, he thanked them. "Words can't express . . . thank you . . . and Merry Christmas! Merry Christmas, everyone!"

Father Powell was conducting the mass in great solemnity. Then he noticed Mrs. Grogen on the hall phone. She broke into a broad grin and held up her hand in an okay sign. Father Powell's face burst into a grin so broad it startled his congregation.

Chapter 30

Kelly Green sat slumped in his chair, looking slightly disheveled. "What Child Is This" streamed over the radio waves.

Dwight entered the broadcast studio carrying a single sheet of wire service copy. His grin indicated he had something up his sleeve.

Kelly took the wire copy, and moved it back and forth as if trying to get it in focus. As he read the copy, he suddenly sat up straight. He reread the news release, stood up, and walked to the window. Snowdrifts buried the cars in the parking lots, and trees drooped under the weight of the snowfall.

"Well, whaddaya know?" he said under his breath. "There's some hope left in this old world after all." Through the open studio door, he yelled, "Hey, Dwight!"

Dwight's voice responded from a distance, "Yeah? What do you need?"

"Merry Christmas, buddy! Merry, reindeer-infested, candy cane-crunching Christmas!"

Dwight stuck his head back in the doorway. Laughing he replied, "Same to you, turkey!"

Kelly returned to his chair, put on his headset, added the last empty Pepsi bottle to the growing pyramid, swept the collection of wadded paper balls out of his way, and reached out to stop the music. With feeling, he keyed the mike. "We interrupt the 'Sounds of Christmas' for this important bulletin . . . "

The Liesels' large, old-fashioned radio was tuned to AM-1220. "A tragedy was averted early this morning when the little boy who had been lost in last night's storm . . ."

The baker and his wife were seated on their couch, dressed in bathrobes, and wrapped in a blanket, listening to the antique radio.

" . . . was found safe and apparently unharmed in spite of his exposure to the elements."

The older couple held each other. Rolf Liesel kissed his wife on the forehead. "You see, Mama? God in his goodness has answered your prayer."

Across town, Kelly's broadcast played on a bedside radio. "The hospital staff was at a loss to explain how the boy, wearing only a lightweight jacket . . ."

Joshua and his mother were seated on the floor listening to the radio. Joshua was still holding his favorite teddy bear.

" . . . could have survived prolonged exposure in sub-freezing temperatures without so much as a case of frostbite."

Joshua turned to his mother excitedly. "Mama! The Lord heard your prayer!" Joshua's mother hugged her son to her, deeply moved by the unfolding news. "And yours too. We mustn't forget that."

Joshua's eyes grew large.

Chapter 31

A Mickey Mouse radio sat on David's dresser. It too was tuned to Kelly's broadcast. "Whatever the cause, the little boy's family, friends, and, permit me to add, this announcer . . . ."

David was fast asleep in his bed. He had a relaxed smile on his face. Whiskers, who was curled up against the boy, sat up and turned her head to one side. She watched as the woman in white, the same woman David had seen at the shopping center, approached his bed. She smiled down at the sleeping boy, the great love evident in her eyes. She leaned over the boy, pulled back the covers, and bent down to give him a kiss.

"... are convinced we've witnessed a Christmas miracle, right here in our own neighborhood. It brought people of different beliefs and different backgrounds together . . . all for the love of a small child. Maybe there's some good left in the world after all. Merry Christmas, everyone, from all of us here at AM-1220."

Whiskers started at the sound of footsteps, as David's dad approached. Mark entered the room and sat on the floor next to his son. The woman in white was gone. Mark watched his son with renewed relief and thanksgiving. He settled in and listened to the radio.

A picture of David's mother sat on the nightstand beside the bed. She appeared to be smiling at her sleeping son.

As Mark listened to the newscast, he noticed something spilling out from under the covers. Absently, he pulled back the covers and discovered a white shawl had been placed over David's shoulders.

The radio resumed playing Christmas carols. Caroline popped her head in the room to say good-bye. Whispering, she expressed her relief. "I can't tell you what it means to me to see him sleeping there, safe and unharmed. I want you to know this was an answer to my prayers. Now I can go home and rest. What a blessing!"

Mark nodded thoughtfully. "It really is a miracle, isn't it?" Then, as an afterthought, he softly touched the shawl. "Is this yours? It's beautiful. I don't think I've ever seen it before."

Caroline moved closer, fingered the shawl, and shook her head slowly. "No, it's not mine. I feel like I've seen it before, but I can't quite place it." Caroline crossed to her brother-in-law and gave him a hug. "I couldn't have wished for a happier outcome. Merry Christmas, Mark."

He held her for just a moment. "Caroline, it really is a Merry Christmas after all."

On David's dresser, a music box sat framed by the window behind it. Through the window, the snow-laden trees presented their own Christmas card display, a breathtaking panorama left by the storm.

As the carol on the radio faded, the figure atop the music box began to turn, and the sound of the radio was replaced by the music box playing "What Child Is This?"

Beside the music box was an arrangement of family pictures. In the center of that arrangement was an old photo of two of David's ancestors on their wedding day. The bride stood beside her new husband. He was a strong, handsome young man dressed in formal wear from that era. His outfit was totally white, from his coat and cravat to his high top shoes. Over the woman's shoulders, in the photograph, was the white lace shawl that now covered David. The brass legend under the picture read "Great-Great-Grandmother and Grandfather Peterson on their wedding day."

As was her habit, Whiskers nuzzled the sleeping boy's ear. Then, purring, she snuggled next to her master, content to sleep until he awoke to the adventures of Christmas Day.

Mills Crenshaw is a successful marketing executive and prominent radio talk show host. His professional writing career began as a ghost writer for one of the popular *Elvis* books. In December 1980, he wrote a short story called "Little Boy Lost," as a Christmas present for his children.

In subsequent years, it became a family tradition for Mills to present a new short story each Christmas Eve. In 1992, a collection of those short stories was published by Quilted Bear Publishing and became an instant success. *The Christmas of '45* is the novel that grew out of these classic short stories.